Unbelievable Crimes Volume Six

Unbelievable Crimes, Volume 6

Daniela Airlie

Published by Daniela Airlie, 2023.

While every precaution has been taken in the preparation of this book, the publisher assumes no responsibility for errors or omissions, or for damages resulting from the use of the information contained herein.

UNBELIEVABLE CRIMES VOLUME SIX

First edition. September 10, 2023.

Copyright © 2023 Daniela Airlie.

Written by Daniela Airlie.

Table of Contents

Unbelievable Crimes Volume Six: Macabre Yet Unknown True Crime Stories 1

Introduction 3

Living Hell 5

Suspect Number One 17

A Dangerous Woman 27

The Belgian Beast 43

Hotel Of Horror 57

Heists And Homicide 65

Merciless Mass Murderer 77

Santa, The Serial Killer 99

Ice Cold Homicide 113

Final Thoughts 121

The right of Daniela Airlie as the publisher and owner of this work has been asserted in accordance with the Copyright, Designs, and Patents Act 1988. No part of this publication may be reproduced in any format without the publisher's prior written consent. This book is for entertainment and informational purposes only.

Although research from various sources has gone into this book, neither the author nor publisher will be held responsible for any inaccuracies. To the best of the author's knowledge, all information within this publication is factually correct and derived from researching these cases thoroughly. The author may offer speculation and/or opinion throughout this book about the cases covered.

Danielaairlie.carrd.co

Introduction

Welcome to the sixth installment of *Unbelievable Crimes*. If you've read previous books in this series, you'll know I'm an avid follower of true crime stories. It's one of my main interests, and I dedicate much of my time to digesting true crime material. My shelves are filled with books on the topic, my audiobook collection is mostly true crime, and my "recommended for you" section on my streaming services is almost always a true crime documentary. Suffice to say, rarely is there a case I've not heard of.

While cases covered in the other volumes had often been well-known to me prior to writing about them, many of the cases in this volume are relatively new to me. Sure, I'd heard of most of them prior to writing, but I was unfamiliar with the story behind the criminal's name.

For example, I vaguely recall reading about the case of Joanna Dennehy, who embarked on a killing spree for no apparent reason. I didn't know the details of the case, but upon researching it and watching several documentaries about it, the case truly shocked me. It left me with more questions than answers, one of them being, how hadn't I learned about this horrific case before? I detail her crimes in this anthology.

Then there's the cold case of murdered teenager Peggy Reber. If you've read other books in this series, you'll know I find cold cases a difficult category of true crime. I find them frustrating to learn about since there is no closure, no arrest, no justice, and no resolution. Cases like this upset me, so no doubt will haunt the friends and families of the victim forever. Reading cases like this leave me with a feeling of defeat. With Peggy's murder being one of those cases that never saw justice, I imagine that's why her story managed to bypass me. In an effort to pay more heed to unsolved cases, I will be covering her brutal murder and the hunt for her killer.

The case of Marc Dutroux managed to evade my attention for years, too, which is surprising considering the barbarity of his crimes. Despite the evil that this man carried out, his crimes aren't well-known, even among the true crime community. Dutroux was a sexual deviant who preyed on young girls, one of the most abhorrent and twisted crimes a person can carry out. I'll cover his sick spate of deviancy and the plight of his young victims.

As I always like to remind you (particularly if some readers are just picking up book six without reading any prior volumes), these books aim to detail lesser-covered true crime stories. The ones with no headline news, little public outrage, or just a small amount of coverage within the true crime community. These crimes should never be forgotten, and the perpetrator's acts should forever be reviled.

And, as I always do, let me remind you that this book contains some crimes that are particularly brutal to learn about. This includes cases involving sexual assault and torture and crimes involving children. Please bear this in mind before delving in.

With that said, if you're ready, let's begin *Volume Six*.

Living Hell

There's one type of crime that makes me shudder. Cases where the victim is kidnapped and held captive in an isolated, uncomfortable place only the abductor knows of. I covered a case like this in *Volume One*. The shocking spate of crimes carried out by James Jamelske saw him take unsuspecting young females from the streets and keep them in his specially-made dungeon underneath his marital home.

The fear, the trauma, and the dread of each day these victims had to endure is terrifying. They never knew which day would be their last. Some lasted months and months in the damp squalor Jamelske kept them in. Their abuser was their only hope in life. The only person who could feed them, bring them water and decide if they make it out alive. Essentially, they lived in a real-life nightmare they could not wake up from.

This case evokes a similar response in me. The victim in this story was held for months in a storage container while being subjected to horrific assaults at the hands of her deranged captor.

Abby Hernandez wasn't even 15 years old when Nathaniel Kibby dragged her into a world of hell. I can't comprehend the emotional agony endured by the girl, but by some miracle, she made it out of her ordeal alive.

Mid-afternoon on a warm October day in 2013, Abby Hernandez was making her way home from school. The teen's hometown of North Conway was nestled in a mountainous area in the state of New Hampshire. Crime, although not unheard of, was rare here.

On the leisurely walk back home, Abby was texting her friend who'd gotten the bus home. Suddenly, after back-and-forth messages, Abby stopped replying. There was no *I'm home, talk to you later*, or *I'm jumping in the shower, speak soon* messages to tell her friend she wouldn't be replying for a while.

Abby's usual routine after school was to unlock the house, let the dogs in the yard to do their business, clean up a little, get herself something quick to eat, and watch some TV. She'd lounge around, texting friends, maybe even speak to them on the phone. Your typical teenage evening routine.

Her mother would arrive home a few hours after Abby since her shifts didn't end until nighttime. When Zenya came home to find the property locked up, she was confused. Had Abby come home and gone back out? After entering the house, she found the dogs hadn't been let out all day. The distressed pets had made clutter and mess, so it was clear that Abby hadn't set foot in the home since she left for school that morning.

Not seeing to the dogs was uncharacteristic of Abby. So was her simply not coming home. The teenager wasn't replying to messages. Her phone was off. Panic set in for the mother, who contacted the police.

When it was daylight, cadaver dogs were sent to retrace Abby's walk home from school. Sure enough, the dogs caught her scent. But it stopped abruptly part-way through her usual route. It looked like the unthinkable had happened - she'd been abducted. Either that or, as the rumor mill was churning out, she had run away after finding out she was pregnant. There was another theory floating about, too, suggesting the girl had met someone online and had taken off with them.

Rumors and speculation at such a critical time in a possible crime can be damaging. To dismiss a missing teen as a "runaway" can cause a blasé attitude towards an investigation. Despite these theories being preferable to the girl having been kidnapped, the police were certain: it was an abduction.

On the October afternoon that Abby went missing, her walk home was somewhat slower than usual. She'd been wearing a new pair of boots, but the footwear wasn't as comfortable as she'd thought when she put them on. The boots had been rubbing on the back of her foot and on her toes. It was clear to those passing by that the girl struggled slightly to walk at a reasonable pace. The throbbing of her blistering feet gave her an awkward limp.

It was also clear to 34-year-old Nathaniel Kibby, who was driving past the teen as she slowly made her way home. Sensing an opportunity - a vulnerable young girl walking alone - he offered Abby a lift to where she was trying to get to. The pain her boots were causing was enough to prompt Abby to accept the lift. Usually, she wouldn't get in a car with a stranger, but she thought he was a Good Samaritan doing her a favor.

Abby gave the man directions to a restaurant near her home. She was clever enough to avoid giving the stranger her real address, especially since she would be home alone for a few hours after being dropped off. The man said he just needed to make one quick stop at a hardware store before dropping her off, which Abby agreed to. After all, her feet were killing her. It was broad daylight, and the man seemed normal enough. She kept telling herself these things but couldn't help feeling uneasy in his presence.

When the man pulled up at the store, Abby decided she'd thank him for the lift, then she'd get out and make her own way home. As she unbuckled her belt, the driver turned nasty. He pulled a gun on the girl. "I'll shoot you if you dare open the door," he threatened. He warned her he'd slit her throat if she made one wrong move. Abby's will to live caused her to buckle her belt right back up.

The attacker wrapped his jacket tightly around his young victim's head so she couldn't see where he was driving her. After taking away the girl's ability to see, he sped off. Part-way through the journey, the abductor realized his captor could see through a small gap in the fabric of his jacket. Out of annoyance and to assert his dominance, the man tasered Abby for this inconvenience. For the young girl, this would be the first of many unprovoked, senseless, and vile attacks at the hands of Nathaniel Kibby.

The man destroyed Abby's phone before arriving at his property to ensure the girl's whereabouts couldn't be traced.

After what felt like hours of being slumped in the car with a jacket wrapped around her face, Abby was taken from the vehicle and thrown into a dark, cold room. She didn't know it at the time, but she'd been placed in a shipping container. Her captor had converted the once-red metal vessel to include a bed and other basic amenities.

Nathaniel tied his victim to the bed before using utility tape to shut her eyes. If this wasn't fear-inducing enough for Abby, the sick captor then placed a motorcycle helmet on her head. He had taken her sight from her, and the helmet prevented her from hearing properly. The reason for this, it seems, was just to invoke fear into Abby. After all, she'd already seen and heard him. Nathaniel was disorienting the girl to fulfill his twisted kicks.

He then forced himself upon Abby. Again, this would be the first of many attacks of this nature. The cruel man would assault, abuse, and torture his victim on a daily basis. Her most basic needs - shelter, food, and water - were all dangled above her by her captor, the same man who would violate her daily. To fight his daily attacks would mean kissing goodbye to these essentials.

Nathaniel never told Abby his name and insisted she call him "Master." The teen girl did as she was told. She knew if she complied, her chances of survival would increase.

Meanwhile, just 30 miles away, her mother was desperately working with the police to find her daughter. Even the FBI had been brought in to help find the missing girl. The North Conway community banded together to comb the area, looking for Abby.

Forests and woodland surrounded the small town, and plenty of people had fallen foul of the dangers of getting lost there. A thorough search was carried out, but nothing was found, not so much as a small clue. Pictures of Abby and missing persons posters were handed out to local businesses, and her face filled the stores of the small town. The Hernandez family was left disheartened when, after weeks, nobody was coming forward with any information.

It was clear the police had no leads, and the case was getting cold. Still, Zenya released a statement to say she still felt her daughter was alive. Perhaps this was just wishful thinking on the mother's part - to consider the alternative would be just too much to bear. Knowingly or not, Zenya was right. A few weeks after her daughter's vanishing, Zenya was elated to come home to a letter from her missing daughter.

The contents of the letter weren't released initially, but it did give the mother renewed hope. Police analysis of the letter found it to be genuine, and the tone and handwriting in the note were familiar to Zenya. It was certainly written by her missing child. But the letter brought up more questions than it offered answers. *Was Abby being held captive? Was she coerced into writing this letter to get authorities to back off?*

Not even in their darkest thoughts could anyone imagine the truth: that Abby was just 45 minutes away in a fortified shipping container. Her existence was now reduced to being abused on a daily basis. Abby hadn't seen sunlight or been able to take in a big breath of fresh air for weeks and weeks.

The teenage girl was losing weight rapidly. Her once glowing skin was now pale and dull. Her face was gaunt. Her eyes, once big and bright, were now haunted and full of fear.

Despite her dire situation, Abby clung to hope. She would pray every day, begging to be allowed freedom once again. In a bid to keep God with her, she never said "Amen" when finishing a prayer. She feared if she did, she'd lose the string of contact she had with Him. While praying, she also didn't want to leave things to chance either. She began plotting ways she could make it out of confinement. The clever teen decided the best way to do this would be to get her abuser on her side.

The girl began engaging in conversation with her captor. "I don't judge you for this, you know," she told him. "If you ever let me go, I wouldn't tell anybody." Slowly but surely, she was gaining Nathaniel's trust. "Everybody makes mistakes; you're not a bad person," she would remind him. Eventually, this plan worked. She was allowed out of the container and was moved into her captor's trailer, parked right next to the container.

It was better than sitting in the dark, cold, metal vessel she'd been confined in for months. While in the trailer, Nathaniel decided to make the girl work for the "luxury" of being let out of her cell. He'd make her print counterfeit money.

Nathaniel Kibby was frequently in trouble with the law. His neighbors and even his landlord steered clear of the man since he was moody and seemed to live for conflict. Despite this, he had managed to hold down a steady job for almost a decade before he was laid off. This drove him to print fake money as a means of getting by, just another criminal activity to add to his expansive list.

Despite letting Abby in his trailer, Nathaniel was still paranoid that the girl might try to escape. So, he installed security cameras around the place to keep a close eye on her. However, these cameras weren't working - it was just another tactic to keep the girl in a state of fear and compliance. He also put a shock collar around her neck and warned her that if she tried to yell to the neighbors for help, he'd push the button and shock her relentlessly.

"Go ahead, raise your voice," Nathaniel prompted Abby the first time he clipped the collar around her neck. As she did, he immediately shocked her, causing the girl to collapse in fear. "Now you know what it feels like; that's what happens if you try anything funny."

The months passed by. Abby was still complying with her abductor while trying to form a bond with him. While he was still abusing her daily, the man began to think Abby's feelings toward him were genuine. That she did like him and that she did care about him. This meant he'd offer her "privileges" such as books to read to pass the time. Unknowingly, this would be his undoing.

Among the random books he gave to his victim, one had a name on the jacket cover. "Nate Kibby."

"Who's Nate Kibby?" Abby asked, presumably not thinking her abuser was stupid enough to hand her a book with his real name written inside. After a pause, Nathaniel asked Abby how she knew his name. After months of being abused by this man, she finally had his name.

Five months after he abducted Abby, the serial criminal was arrested for assaulting a woman after a minor road accident. While in police custody, Abby was stuck in the container. I can only imagine what would become of the teenage girl if her abductor had been arrested for something more serious and was kept in custody. No doubt the man wouldn't have told the police he had a girl locked away in his property, and she'd have suffered an agonizing death.

Up until that summer, things remained the same for the criminal and his victim. Abby's days were spent being abused, printing money, and doing her best to befriend the man simultaneously keeping her alive and making her existence unbearable.

Nathaniel didn't have much in the way of human connection. He had few friends and certainly nobody who took an interest in him. This is where Abby found she could gain some kind of advantage in the bleak situations she was in. When the teen asked how he was, empathized with him, and showed compassion toward him, he bought it. Abby was doing what she had to in order to survive. The hope of being reunited with her mother never left her.

In July 2014, Nathaniel got a phone call from a woman he'd given some of his counterfeit money to. The money was to pay the sex worker for her services, and when she tried to spend some of the notes at a store, the cashier figured the money was fake and called the police.

The woman was arrested and gave officers Kibby's name as the source of the fake cash. After being questioned, the woman called Nathaniel and warned him that police were on their way to bust him, so he better get rid of any incriminating evidence. Little did the woman know, it wasn't just printing fake money the man was guilty of: he was a rapist, violent abuser, and perverse predator.

Panicked by the call, Nathaniel swung into action and cleaned the trailer top to bottom with the help of Abby. All evidence of his illegal hustle was gotten rid of. Now, there was just the issue of what he was going to do with Abby. There seemed to be just two options. Kill her or let her go. If the teenager hadn't spent the past nine months gaining the trust of her abductor, there's a high chance he'd have chosen the former. Thankfully, Nathaniel chose to let Abby go.

On July 20, 2014, the man dropped her off where he snatched her the year prior. After he drove off, Abby couldn't help but laugh. She was elated. She was free. Despite the horrors she'd endured, a smile was plastered across her face the whole way home. She couldn't believe she was free; a big part of her had resigned to a life living in the container. Finally, she could say, "Amen."

Her mother got the shock of her life when she saw her daughter. It was definitely Abby, but not the Abby she remembered. She was very thin and unkempt, and her eyes were full of sorrow. Still, her daughter was home. She was alive. Zenya could barely believe it.

The police were called, and the teen girl told them everything she knew - except the name of her captor. Even the description she offered officers was only somewhat of a resemblance to her abductor. It could have been fear that stopped her from passing over all the details. After all, Nathaniel threatened the life of Abby's mother and her dogs if she told anyone what he'd done.

In the end, Abby confessed to her mother that she knew the name of her attacker. She made her mother promise not to go to the police with this information. Of course, it would break your heart to break a promise you made to your child, but in instances like this, it's a must. Zenya went to the police with the name Nathaniel Kibby. He was already known to police as a serial menace with a penchant for violent behavior, so they knew where to find him immediately. He was quickly arrested, and his trailer was searched.

The stun gun, the zip ties, the dog collar, and the security camera used in his reign of terror were found.

The criminal was facing 205 charges, every single one of which he denied. When it became apparent the odds were stacked against him, Nathaniel took a plea deal: accept his guilt of aggravated sexual assault, kidnapping, witness tampering, and criminal threatening, and he would get 45 to 90 years in prison. This is exactly what the twisted man got, and it means, more likely than not, he'll die behind bars.

Abby penned an impact statement, which was read out at her abductor's sentencing. In it, she said she'd been living in fear since he carried out repeated rapes and assaults on her. She told him he put himself in jail when he decided to kidnap and abuse her. She ended her statement with hope by acknowledging how she now appreciates life more than ever and that sunshine and fresh air are things she'll never take for granted.

Now, Abby has a son, a stable career, and a life filled with love. She's still on her path to healing, but despite everything Nathaniel Kibby took from her, she has something he'll never have again: freedom.

Suspect Number One

I recall, years ago, watching a true crime documentary - I can't for the life of me recollect the documentary name, but I remember it being a series - about a cold case. In this episode, a woman was killed, and the husband was the main suspect. This isn't anything out of the ordinary. The first person police look at in a homicide case is always the victim's partner.

But, in the program I was watching, the amount of evidence against the deceased's husband was overwhelming. The only piece of evidence they *didn't* have was CCTV footage of the man actually carrying out the murder. Investigators had just about every bit of evidence you'd think you needed to secure a guilty verdict against the man.

Still, the man was exonerated. The not guilty verdict came as quite a shock, considering the plethora of evidence against him.

This case has a familiar feel to it. It's a cold case, but it only has one suspect, and the evidence against them is compelling, to say the least. Patricia Adkins vanished in late June 2001 after finishing work. She's never been seen since, but the crumbs of evidence left suggest foul play at the hands of one person in particular.

Patti, as she was affectionately known, lived in Marysville, Ohio. Crime rates are low, the people are friendly, and the streets are lined with maple trees. It's a quiet suburban area popular with young families. Patti, a single mother of one, lived with her 7-year-old little girl. She'd endured a rough divorce in the late 90s but found herself on good terms with her ex-husband when they figured it was the best way to co-parent their daughter.

Patti had a stable job with a good income. It helped that she was sensible with money, and she spent a decade saving up for a rainy day. Her role at the car factory as a supervisor of the assembly line was a position she excelled at, and she was hoping to move further up the career ladder. Patti got the job in the early 90s, a time when you could expect a job to be for life, and that's just what it was going to be for the ambitious young woman.

Her personal life was somewhat on the up, too, but the man she was seeing wasn't exactly available. In fact, he was completely off the market since he was married. Any reservations Patti had about this disappeared when he told her he'd leave his wife. She truly believed the man when he assured her he had every intention of leaving his marriage to set up a life with her.

But, the man, who has never been named, seemingly never had an intention of leaving his spouse or children.

Patti had been introduced to her lover when the pair became co-workers years prior. It wasn't the best-kept secret at the car factory; their other co-workers guessed something was going on. From intimate lunch breaks to playing cards together, it was clear the pair were close - certainly closer than most people tend to get with those they work with.

Years rolled by, and the man never did leave his wife. In fact, Patti and the man she viewed as her boyfriend never did much, if anything, together outside the confines of the car factory. Her lover said that his wife couldn't find out about the affair. If she did, he'd be financially ruined. He had a side hustle going on besides his work on the assembly line - he ran an auto repair shop. His wife owned half of this business.

Patti's lover confided in her about this and all of his other familial woes. He was unhappy, and marriage wasn't what he thought it would be. He was miserable.

What if he could buy his wife out of the business? Would that make the divorce easier? It didn't take long for Patti to begin asking her lover these questions. And it didn't take long for him to begin accepting money from the woman he would ignore if he saw her while out and about with his family.

As I mentioned, Patti was good with her money. She saved, was careful with how she spent, and made sure she had a solid nest egg for herself and her child. Until her lover needed help, that is, and over a short period of time, she managed to give him $90,000 of her hard-earned cash. It was taken without much hesitation, and she was assured she'd get it back. How and when weren't discussed.

Patti was open about the relationship with those closest to her, her sisters. While they disagreed with their sibling's lifestyle choice, they could see that Patti genuinely adored her boyfriend. *He was in an unhappy marriage*, she stressed to them, and noted he was kind, loving, and the perfect person for her. While they weren't allowed to meet their sister's boyfriend, they took her word that it was all going to end happily. "He'd never harm one hair on my head," Patti insisted.

In June 2001, Patty told her sister that she was planning a vacation with her lover. They were going to Canada, where he'd rented a cabin. The trip was to take place on June 29, and Patti would meet her lover straight after work when her shift ended at midnight. He'd even told her not to pack any clothing - he'd treat her to some when they were on their getaway.

Their meet-up after work was a strange one, though. The plan wasn't for Patti to jump into her lover's truck and for them to head straight to the romantic cabin he'd booked. Instead, she'd jump into the back of the truck and hide underneath a waterproof cover. This was because her lover always dropped a colleague off after his shift, and breaking that routine may cause suspicion for the secret lovers. Patti did as instructed, curling up into a ball in the back of her boyfriend's truck, carrying only a small bag filled with seductive nightwear.

Patti had already warned those close to her that she'd be uncontactable while on vacation. The cabin was remote, there was no phone signal, and they were miles away from a town or payphone. She'd call them when she arrived home the following Saturday, she promised. She told her sister, who was looking after Patti's little girl, she'd collect the child on Sunday. She was also due to pick her cats up from boarding the same day.

Patti would never make it back to her little family.

In fact, it seems she never made it to the cabin in Canada.

It's still uncertain if she ever even made it out of the parking lot of her workplace.

The day after Patti was due home, her sister rang her. The call rang through to voicemail. She tried again. And again. Perhaps they weren't back yet, the concerned woman thought. In reality, she was just trying to console herself - she knew something sinister was at play. Patti would never just leave her daughter and beloved pets without getting in touch.

By Sunday evening, her sister decided to make a call to Patti's lover's home. Sure, this would anger the mother-of-one, but the worried sister had to do something. The cheating husband's wife answered the phone and advised her that her other half wasn't there. A missing person's report was created by the Marysville Police Department at the request of Patti's anxious family.

Meanwhile, the sister tried Patti's lover's home phone again. This time, he answered. He denied knowing a "Patti" and pleaded ignorance to having been having an affair with the woman for years. It was a strange thing to deny, considering Patti was his superior at work. While he may not have wanted to drop himself in it by admitting to an affair while his wife was perhaps in earshot, it was no secret that he knew a Patti - he worked with one. He had hundreds of lunch breaks with her over the years. He joked with her in front of co-workers. Many of them knew they were having an affair.

Still, when Patti Adkins' sister called about her being missing for a week, the man didn't decide to come clean. He had no concern a woman was missing, not to mention it was the same woman he'd promised to leave his wife for. He had no answers to any questions thrown his way.

With the police now involved, the unnamed lover of Patti's was suspect number one. Two days after the missing person's report was filed, investigators interviewed the man, who was quick to deny any kind of extramarital affair with his colleague. They were acquaintances at best, he would explain, and that any suggestion they were due to go on vacation was simply untrue.

The man perhaps didn't bank on Patti disclosing much of their relationship to her sisters. They knew a lot, despite the man insisting Patti keep their relations secret, even from those she loved. They knew their sister had given this man close to $100,000 over the years and felt the outcome was a result of Patti's trusting nature. He'd got what he wanted and disposed of her when she wanted more from him, the Adkins sisters surmised.

Three days after speaking with the suspect, police issued a warrant to search his home. The man didn't seem fazed by this and put up no resistance when officers requested full access to his house and business. They wouldn't find anything incriminating, but investigators would happen upon items that confirmed the man certainly was having an affair with Patti.

He'd kept a letter his lover wrote him, professing her desire to be with him properly. The letter spoke of their relationship at length, so it wasn't like Patti had penned the man a one-sided love letter. Not only that, he'd kept gifts his girlfriend had given him: a novelty t-shirt she'd bought him while with her sister, who corroborated the shirt was certainly a gift from her sister. They also recovered a mobile phone gifted by Patti.

A search of Patti's property found it untouched from the day she left for work. She hadn't returned. Her car was still parked in the garage. Her bank cards hadn't been used since before she was due to head out on vacation. The bag she packed for the special trip was never recovered, and neither were the contents.

The finger of blame was pointing heavily toward Patti's lover, but the police had nothing but circumstantial evidence. A lot of it, but nonetheless, circumstantial. They needed more to secure an arrest. In their search for concrete evidence tying the man to the disappearance of the young mother, they scoured his truck for DNA evidence. In doing so, they noticed he'd bought a brand new truck cover. Was this to rid his truck of incriminating forensic evidence?

This was an interesting - yet another circumstantial - piece of information. After a thorough search, forensics couldn't find any of Patti's DNA in the man's truck. But they did find yet another piece of implicative evidence - cat hair from one of Patti's cats. The hair was proven to be from the missing woman's pet since investigators obtained a sample from the felines for analysis. This would, again circumstantially, place Patti in the back of the man's vehicle.

There was also a minuscule spot of blood recovered from the back of the truck. The blood, sadly, was too small for an accurate analysis to confirm if the droplet belonged to Patti. There is still hope that the advances in DNA testing will someday be able to conclusively confirm whether or not the blood was Patti's, but as of writing, these technological advancements haven't been made.

Still, there was more indirect evidence for investigators to discover. When the boyfriend left work the day Patti vanished, he did so with a co-worker as his passenger. The pair often carpooled, and this day was no different. According to the co-worker, he and the suspect left work just after midnight, driving forty minutes to grab some post-work food. The pair settled for a burger drive-through to be eaten in the car while listening to the radio and driving home.

This is where things get interesting, though. Both men say they sat in the drive-through for almost an hour before getting their food. The manager on duty rejected this claim, saying he checked the till and noticed only a few orders had been taken between midnight and 2 a.m. There were so few orders that the manager estimated there would only have been a few minutes - if any - wait for patrons to get their food and go.

Patti's lover didn't get home until 2:30 a.m. that morning, as confirmed by his wife, two and a half hours after finishing his shift.

So what were the boyfriend and his friend doing in the spare time they had? If, as the burger joint employee suggested, the men had their food and were on their way within a few minutes, where else had the pair gone?

Things were looking more and more incriminating for Patti's lover. He completed a lie detector test at the request of investigators, which he subsequently failed. As you'll likely know, the results of lie detector tests can't be used in court, so this led nowhere. Still, it's an interesting aspect of the case. You may wonder why he would have taken the lie detector if he was guilty. It's a good question. But why did the man deny an affair with Patti yet retain love letters in his home for police to find?

News got around the car factory where Patti worked. Everyone knew she'd been in an illicit relationship with the suspect. All eyes were on him whenever he turned up for his night shift, something that likely prompted him to quit his assembly line job shortly after the news of Patti's vanishing.

Years passed with no leads, no new evidence, and no word from Patti. Some have suggested the mother-of-one simply took off and began a new life. Perhaps these people were trying to offer a misguided glimmer of hope to the Adkins family that their beloved Patti is still around somewhere. However, in 2006, the missing woman was officially declared dead.

The boyfriend remained married and hasn't been charged with any involvement in Patti's disappearance.

A Dangerous Woman

Women who kill purely for the thrill of it aren't common. The majority of serial killers are men, and even most female spree killers are often in cahoots with a male accomplice. The case of Joanna Dennehy is unlike just about every other tale of a female murderer - she killed simply because she enjoyed it. The crime spree she embarked on flipped the script entirely on what we could expect from women who kill.

She had male accomplices. She carried out the killings herself, armed with a hunting knife. The people she preyed on were solely men. She even maneuvered one of her deceased victims into a sick sexual pose after slaughtering him. Everything we've come to expect from men in the world of true crime, Joanna Dennehy grabbed hold of and took to a shocking extreme.

Born in 1982, Dennehy grew up near St. Albans, a historic city north of London, England. Her childhood, according to those who knew her during her younger and teen years, was filled with love and support. Kathleen and Kevin Dennehy encouraged their daughter and her sister Maria to aim for good grades and participate in school activities. Young Dennehy did as much and was noted as being an excellent pupil who was easy to teach.

However, teenagehood loomed, and it wasn't going to be good for the Dennehy family.

Joanna began hanging around with other teens who were deemed undesirable by those who cared about the girl. With her newfound crowd, some of whom were much older than her, Joanna began drinking, taking drugs, and flouting her curfew. She was having more than a typical teen rebellion, though; she was taking her rule-breaking to extremes. Her parents despaired, unsure how they could get their daughter back on the straight and narrow. Sadly, they never would.

Around the age of 15, Joanna decided she'd had enough of being told what to do. She moved out of the family home to live with her newfound companions, most of whom didn't have jobs and substituted their lack of work with criminal endeavors.

The environment she found herself in was a melting pot of petty criminals, those procuring and selling drugs, and heavy drinkers. It was around this time she'd meet her long-term boyfriend, John Treanor, who was 20 years old. Joanna was around 15 at this time, so she was below the age of consent in the U.K., although some outlets have suggested her relationship with John didn't begin until she turned 16.

Still, a four-year age gap is a lot when you're young. The difference between a 16-year-old and a 20-year-old is vast despite the gap not being too great. At those ages, you want different things, are able to do different things, and have different needs. Whereas John could drink alcohol legally and was old enough to pass his driving test, Joanna was too young for either - legally, at least. She should have been sitting her exams at school, readying herself for further education, but she gave up going to school altogether.

Two years into the relationship, at the age of 17, Joanna discovered she was pregnant. This wasn't welcome news for Dennehy - she was adamant that she didn't want children. Not then, not ever.

Still, she went ahead with the pregnancy and gave birth to a little girl. Despite Dennehy being so young, this could have been a cornerstone for her. A time for her to reconsider her antics, to begin and take care of herself and be better for her baby. This wouldn't be the case.

As soon as she was discharged from the hospital, Dennehy began abusing drugs and alcohol. Looking back, you can perhaps pity the young mother. She'd just given birth to a child she'd never wanted, and although she felt love for her baby, she was struggling with her world being turned upside down after the new arrival demanded much of her time and attention. She could have been suffering from postnatal depression, coupled with the irking thought that motherhood simply wasn't for her.

After all, Dennehy enjoyed getting high, cans of lager, packets of cigarettes, and any drug that was being handed around that day... all activities you clearly can't do with a baby attached to your hip.

Still, it was noted that the young mother would partake in these activities anyway. She'd also begin self-harming, something her boyfriend noticed quite quickly. It was hard for him not to - the young woman was slicing at her belly, leaving large gashes where the blade opened her skin. Where a knife wasn't freely available to do damage to her body, she'd use razor blades.

Still, in 2005, she would give birth again. Her behavior hadn't improved from the first pregnancy, and if anything, Dennehy would only get worse the second time around. By this point, the woman was addicted to alcohol, and all of her relationships had just about crumbled into nothingness.

She'd developed a strong dislike for her parents. She distanced herself from her sister. She'd spent a great deal of time arguing with the father of her children, to the point she'd begun abusing him during her drunken rages.

The pair ended up in a council bungalow in Cambridgeshire, but despite the calming atmosphere of the university town, Dennehy wouldn't settle down or quit drugs or drink. It was here that the neighbors were regular witnesses to the young woman's violent rages, often targeted at John. At one point, Dennehy took a cricket bat and pummeled her partner with the makeshift weapon. As John lay in a ball on the floor, his partner was raining blows on him, yelling all the while. It wasn't uncommon to see John running errands with black eyes or bruises on his face. It was common knowledge to those in the area that the man was a victim of domestic abuse.

The neighbors also noticed a stark difference between the couple. John was mild, polite, and considered an approachable individual in the quiet community. Joanna, however, was the complete opposite.

It was clear the young woman was frequently under the influence of drink or drugs, or both. On one occasion, the mother even shaved one of her daughter's heads in a drunken act that was later explained as the mother trying to rid her child of nits. However, the explanation for shaving the child's long locks wasn't believed, and it was surmised that Dennehy had again acted out in a fit of drunkenness.

Her alcohol-fueled behavior was well-known. She'd take off from the family home for days, sometimes weeks, at a time. When she arrived home, unkempt, unclean, and full of illicit substances, she'd never tell John where she'd been or who with. She didn't keep her affairs with other men too secret, though, as their neighbors spotted Dennehy with men in suggestive situations.

It was noted by neighbors that John was the primary caregiver for his and Dennehy's two daughters. He'd get them ready for school, drop them off, pick them up, and was the parent who offered the most stability and positive attention. Dennehy rarely did anything with her children, not even offering the most basic parenting skills. If she wasn't off with other partners, she was drinking in the town center, where she'd often get in fights.

Eventually, John had enough of the physical abuse. His daughters were getting older and were privy to the relationship he had with their mother: full of animosity, abuse, and violence. He packed up and took his children three hours away to Glossop. Dennehy wasn't able to keep the cottage they'd been living in and moved 15 miles away to the city of Peterborough.

She would continue her path of iniquity here, carrying out what would later be called "The Peterborough Ditch Murders."

Around this time, she found herself behind bars for stealing, during which time she was admitted to hospital. While she was here, doctors diagnosed the woman with antisocial personality disorder and OCD. It's unclear if she got any treatment for this or if she refused to accept any help. During her short stint in jail, she would have been forced to give up her proclivity for drugs and drink. At the very least, she would have had no access to her addictions, leaving her with time to clear her mind and make use of the prison's rehab facilities.

While in jail, she was sent to a psychiatrist who had some interesting discoveries. She had a condition that meant she enjoyed hurting people; by doing so, she got a sexual thrill. It's called "paraphilia sadomasochism" and is a rare condition for females. It rang true for Dennehy - she did enjoy inciting pain on others, as well as receiving pain in return.

Dennehy also began bragging that she'd killed multiple times - claims that were untrue - to boost her notoriety in jail. It's unclear if this was done out of fear to scare off the hardened lifers in there, which seems unlikely, or because she wanted it to be true.

Upon her release, she was back to her old ways in a heartbeat. Just 12 months after her jail sentence for theft, she embarked on a killing spree with her accomplice, Gary Stretch. Ironically, he towered at 7 foot 3 inches tall.

She moved into a new property, where she began an intimate relationship with her landlord, Kevin Lee. Her location had changed, but just about everything else stayed the same: the boozing, the drug taking, and the sex in return for money.

Kevin was a 48-year-old dad and husband. His business was renting rooms out of one of his properties to those on a low income or those unable to be housed elsewhere. When he met Joanna, he offered her a place to stay, and before long, a sexual relationship ensued. Dennehy told her new landlord that she'd just been released from an eight-year stint in jail for killing her rapist father. It was a complete fabrication, but Kevin bought it.

With this in mind, Kevin also found other uses for the aggressive woman and would use her intimidation skills to threaten other tenants who were behind on their rent. It was a role Dennehy excelled at. The fear she made people feel gave her a twisted kick.

Dennehy had a life she relished. Her own place, surrounded by those who liked drink and drugs as much as she did, and some money coming in via benefits.

As well as her dalliances with Kevin, Dennehy also embarked on a relationship with 31-year-old Lucasz Slaboszewski, a Polish national who had moved to Peterborough in search of a job. After the pair met, it didn't take long for them to get intimate. Lucasz, not knowing Dennehy wasn't the type to be tied down, felt as if he was in a relationship with his new love interest. For Dennehy, Lucasz was just another man to seduce. As well as Kevin and Lucasz, Dennehy was also sleeping with Gary Stretch.

In mid-March 2013, Lucasz was elated to receive a text message from his lover, asking him to visit her bedsit, promising booze and a good time. The man, who had taken more than a keen liking to Dennehy, didn't need to be asked twice. As agreed, the pair enjoyed copious amounts of booze and each other's company. Dennehy was certainly enjoying it - she knew exactly what she was doing and why she'd invited Lucasz there in the first place. She was going to end his life. *Why?* Because she wanted to make her violent, bloody thoughts a reality.

Under the guise of a sexual encounter, Dennehy blindfolded her lover before reaching for her hunting knife. Without hesitation, the woman pierced the sharp blade through the man's chest, penetrating his heart. The victim was in a vulnerable position and died before he had a chance to overpower his attacker.

The kill satisfied Dennehy's lust for blood, for a short while at least. After the murder, she was faced with the inconvenience of moving the body. Dennehy was tough, there was no doubt about that, but disposing of a body wasn't something she felt she had the strength to do. Plus, she didn't have a car, and dragging a corpse through the Peterborough streets to dump it wasn't a good idea. So, she enlisted the help of her lover, Gary Stretch.

Stretch, much like Lucasz, was enamored by Dennehy. He was like a big puppy around her, doing whatever she asked of him. Even disposing of a dead body and covering up her murder. Stretch brought a friend along with him to help move Lucasz's body. It's a concerning notion that both men weren't fazed by the bloodied, lifeless man laid in Dennehy's flat. They simply did as she instructed, bundled the dead man into Stretch's car, and drove the corpse to the quiet countryside. Here, the two men callously dragged the body from the trunk and flung it on the side of a country road.

With the killing complete and the body disposed of, Dennehy's rush was fizzling out. The lust for blood was once again consuming her, and she wanted nothing more than to recreate the thrill of murder. It was just a question of who and when. It took Dennehy just nine days after the first murder to come up with a plan: she'd kill another tenant from the building she lived in.

His name was John Chapman. It seems Dennehy targeted him in a calculated, predatory way. John was an alcoholic who didn't stray too far from his room. He was a war veteran without any close family. He didn't have friends who would come check up on him. In a nutshell, it would take a while for anyone to notice the 56-year-old had vanished.

On March 28, 2013, Dennehy made her way from her room to John's and knocked on the door. She took alcohol with her to secure an invite into the man's abode. Dennehy was unsure if he'd let her in since she'd been threatening him to move out of the room after failing to pay rent. The woman wasn't exactly pleasant when enforcing an eviction, so to say John was wary of Dennehy is an understatement. In fact, he was likely afraid of her. He was known as a friendly, harmless drunk, the complete opposite of the woman knocking on his door and offering him some beers.

The man had fallen on hard times, but this didn't bother Dennehy. If anything, it worked in her favor since he accepted her offer of free booze.

Once inside her soon-to-be victim's room, she opened a drink with him and shared a conversation with the lonely man. One drink became another, then another. Dennehy, while drinking, paced herself, making sure she'd be fit enough to slaughter him once he was drunk enough. Hours passed by before John eventually succumbed to the strong beer he'd been given. He fell into a slumber, and Dennehy stood above him, knife in hand. It was the same knife she'd used in her first murder.

This time, Dennehy's violence escalated. She rained blow after blow onto the incapacitated man's neck and chest, creating a grotesque bloodbath as she ended John Chapman's life. There was zero chance of survival for the man, the attack was just too brutal.

Again, the killer enlisted the help of her friend-slash-lover, Gary Stretch. The pair dumped the war veteran's brutalized body in the same countryside area as Lucasz Slaboszewski. It's unclear if Dennehy and her accomplices just didn't care that they'd get caught or if they wanted to get caught. Their behavior could suggest carelessness since they were sloppy in covering up their tracks.

The intensity of the killing saw Dennehy quickly want to recreate that high. Just mere hours after stabbing John Chapman to death, she voiced her desire to find another man to slay. Again, it was just a question of who.

The following day, March 29, Dennehy invited her landlord lover over to her room. Kevin Lee was thought of highly within the community, offering his bedsits at low rates for those who'd fallen on hard times. He was also known to be lax with his background checks, offering accommodation to those who would normally be rejected. His kind nature was something Dennehy took advantage of, and by all accounts, it seemed like Kevin was in awe of Dennehy's domineering presence and confidence.

The lovers enjoyed a day of drinking, which led to some drunken games, one of which saw Dennhey ask Kevin to put one of her dresses on. To Kevin, it was harmless fun. For Dennehy, it was a twisted addition to her murderous plan. Once he was in the dress, the woman picked up her knife and began pummeling her lover's chest with the blade. Kevin bled to death, and again, Stretch came to take care of the body.

This disposal had a sick twist. The pair drove the body not too far from where the other two had been left and disposed of Kevin on a country road. Dennehy would pose the body in a humiliating way, leaving Kevin face-first in the dirt with his bottom raised up. He was still wearing the dress he was murdered in.

The drive away from Kevin's body was filled with joking and laughter from Dennehy. She found it funny that her latest kill would be found in such a degrading pose. The fact that Kevin was a husband and father didn't matter to the murderer; the man had served his purpose, and she couldn't wait for him to be found.

There hadn't been much care or thought put into where the killer and her minions left the bodies, so it wasn't long before one was discovered by a passerby. Kevin Lee was found the day after he was coldly dumped by the roadside.

Three innocent men lost their lives in just under two weeks at the hands of a woman with an unquenchable thirst for murder. As you can imagine, Dennehy wouldn't be stopping anytime soon. She had to get caught before she gave up her bloody hobby.

Dennehy and Stretch then embarked on a road trip to Norfolk. The plan was for the woman to take as many lives along the way as she could. Meanwhile, the police were on the hunt for Kevin's killer, and Dennehy was a prime suspect. She was nowhere to be found, however. The woman wasn't known for committing crimes covertly, so it wouldn't be long for police to catch up with her. Sadly, she'd manage to have more "fun," as she described the act of killing, before authorities snared her.

On April 2, Dennehy and her sidekick carried out a robbery with the intent of selling the stolen goods for cash. The money would fund their murderous road trip, fueled by drink and a lust to kill. Nine was Dennehy's desired minimum kill count. All men, no women, and no children. The only rules she seemed to have. Stretch was happy to help his sometimes lover achieve this.

With a car full of stolen goods, the pair needed a buyer for them. Stretch got in touch with a man he knew would be interested, Mark Lloyd. They arranged to meet, and the goods were exchanged for cash. Before Dennehy took off on her killing spree, though, she couldn't help but boast to Mark about the murders she'd just carried out. Mark, who simply wanted to acquire some ill-gotten goods from his old friend, found himself in a tricky situation. Not only had Dennehy confessed to murder, but he ended up in the back of Stretch's car, unable to get out. He didn't want to act too disgusted by what Dennehy had admitted in case he was victim number four.

Instead, he sat rigid in the back seat as the two criminals in the front laughed about the killings, the disposals, and the way Dennehy would slaughter future victims. "I want to have my fun," she confided in Mark. "I'm a killer."

He could think of nothing else to do except agree with the crazed woman sitting before him.

The group reached Norfolk, where they noticed a man walking the street. The unassuming 64-year-old barely had a chance to comprehend what was going on before Stretch hit the brakes on the car, allowing Dennehy to run out and ram her knife into the man. She then raced back to the car, and the trio sped off.

Perhaps Dennehy thought she'd got the man in his heart. This was her favorite technique, going by her previous kills. Luckily for Robin Bereza, the woman wounded his shoulder, and his injury wasn't life-threatening. Still, after the attack, he fell to the floor, blood gushing from his lesion, looking around for help.

Meanwhile, Dennehy and Stretch were laughing maniacally as they sped the streets of Norfolk. The woman wanted another victim immediately, so when they saw 57-year-old John Rogers and his dog, Dennehy said he was the one. Stretch pulled up as instructed, and the woman exited the car. She brazenly walked up to the man, who would have no clue this stranger had such evil intentions for him and began stabbing him.

She was far more ferocious this time. The attack was frenzied, and John suffered over 40 wounds at the hands of his attacker. When Dennehy was done, she calmly walked back to the getaway vehicle. For good measure, she stole the man's dog. The three of them, plus the dog, again sped the streets. "Let's take him for a walk," Dennehy exclaimed, referring to the dog who no doubt simply wanted to return to his owner.

Dennehy, despite her penchant for violence, treated the dog with care for the duration he was with her. Thankfully, though, the police were onto her, and her reign of terror looked close to being ended abruptly.

The attacks on the two men had been reported to the police. Luckily, both men survived, and their reports gave police a link to the murder of Kevin Lee. Their attacker had a tattoo of a star on her face, a distinguishing feature that confirmed Dennehy was the woman they were after.

Stretch's speeding car was pulled over, and the three were arrested. Surprisingly, Dennehy was in good spirits. More than this, she was chatty, polite, and engaged with police officers without any restraint. As she was brought to the cells to be detained, she began singing joyfully, surprising the officers who were tasked with guiding her there.

The police were still unaware of the fact Dennehy had killed two more men. She'd been detained for two attempted murders and the murder of Kevin Lee. Lucasz Slaboszewski and John Chapman had been discovered by the point, but the link hadn't yet been made to Dennehy. It wouldn't take long, though, since the woman used the same knife in each attack.

Not only that, John lived in the same property as her, and there were incriminating messages to Lucasz from Dennehy's phone. There was no way she could deny the murders, although it was expected she'd plead not guilty at her trial in November 2013.

It was a shock when she took the stand and announced to all she was the killer. The team representing her asked her to reconsider, but she insisted she was guilty and claimed she regretted nothing. Mark Lloyd testified against the killer and wasn't charged with aiding Dennehy.

Gary Stretch, however, received a life sentence for his role in the murders. Leslie Layton, another accomplice who helped dispose of the victims, got 14 years behind bars.

Joanna Dennehy got a whole life term for her crimes. As of writing, she is the third woman in the UK to receive this sentence. Like fellow lifers Rosemary West and Myra Hindley, she is deemed too dangerous ever to be released. She relishes in her title of "Britain's Most Dangerous Woman."

The Belgian Beast

When you think of the worst subcategories of criminals, child abusers are up there. Without a doubt, they cause us to feel an innate inner rage. Even other violent criminals despise them.

Two types of crime really rile me up: crimes against children and crimes involving animals. Of course, all crimes bother me, but when it's inflicted on the defenseless who have no voice, it enrages me all the more.

I seethe about the perpetrators of such crimes - weak, pathetic individuals - needing to pick a vulnerable victim to satisfy their deviancy. *How tragically inadequate do you need to be to choose the most helpless in society to be your victim?*

Still, when I hear about these crimes, I must read about them. Often, I will want to scroll past the headline or turn the page, knowing that after reading about such crimes, I'll be angry. But, then, I'd be ignorant of the horrors that go on in this world, and that's not the person I want to be. Would it make my day easier not to read about horrific crimes? Probably, yes. But do I want to live a life of ignorant bliss? No, I don't.

The following crime is certainly anger-inducing. It details the crimes of Marc Dutroux, a truly heinous individual whose depravity defies belief.

Dutroux was born on November 6, 1956, in Ixelles, Belgium. His youth was plagued with crime and delinquency, with his rap sheet of petty crimes becoming quite lengthy by the time he became a man. Also, by this point, his crimes were escalating in their severity. He made it his mission to acquire as much as he could by any means necessary. He would sell women for sex, with their agreement or not, and steal cars to sell.

This nefarious way of making money saw him become extremely comfortable financially. He'd reinvest his ill-gotten gains into property. His trained profession was as an electrician, but illegal activities proved much more fruitful for Dutroux. He managed to marry but refused to settle down, juggling multiple mistresses alongside his wife. One of them was Michelle Martin, a woman he'd go on to marry after his first wife divorced him. The couple would have three children together. The fact Michelle had children with Dutroux is frightening since she was all too aware of his depraved desires.

Dutroux spent much of the '80s kidnapping and raping women. Some of these abductions saw him enlist the help of his wife. He also had an accomplice, Jean van Peteghem, who would carry out these sick deeds. The women were kept for a day, sometimes more, and were brutally raped and tortured before being set free.

Peteghem would talk too much in front of the victims and give away much information about his true identity. This allowed the women to run to the police with tangible evidence about their abductions. In the mid-80s, the trio were arrested.

The victims were all teenagers, apart from one. Her name was Sylvie, and she was just 11 years old. In total, there were seven girls they'd kidnapped and raped, although two of these were unable to be successfully identified.

Michelle Dutroux was charged with being an accomplice to confining the girls and aiding in their sexual abuse. She was given just five years in jail but served less than half this time. Jean van Peteghem received just over six years. Marc Dutroux, the cruelest and most sadistic of the bunch, was given 13 years.

Jail time didn't do anything to quell Dutroux's criminal side. As well as a sexual deviant, he was a liar and a fraud. He managed to convince the prison psychiatrist that he wasn't simply deranged, but instead, he was mentally unwell. As a result, he was prescribed strong sedatives, although the sneaky man never took them. He pocketed them for another day, with some depraved uses in mind for them.

The criminal also managed to gain government assistance of $1,200 a month due to his fictitious mental health problems. The government knew he had more than a handful of properties and wasn't exactly destitute, but he was entitled to the aid nonetheless. Dutroux took it with both hands.

Unbelievably, he was released in 1992, with his good behavior being cited as the reason. He was reunited with his wife/accomplice, and the duo began planning their next round of abductions, rapes, and, this time, murders.

This time, they were going to be more careful. Dutroux got to work building a dungeon in the cellar of a house he owned in Marcinelle, Belgium. The cellar was only 7 feet long and 5 feet high. It was fortified with a heavy concrete door with its own sliding mechanism. Inside the tiny cellar, the sick man placed cage bars, further restricting the movement of the victims he intended to hide there.

The summer of 1995 saw the torture cellar put to use by Dutroux. He abducted eight-year-olds Julie Lejeune and Melissa Russo off the streets as they played before throwing them into his cold, dark dungeon. What began as a day of running around the woods, talking about school, and enjoying the pleasant weather ended in a way neither girl could ever conjure in their worst nightmares. Their innocence, humanity, and lives would be snatched from them horrifically. It wouldn't be quick, either. Dutroux held the girls in his makeshift dungeon for months. They would endure heartbreaking abuse, torture, and sexual assaults.

He would make a number of videotapes of these vile crimes, which he profited from. This aspect of Dutroux's crimes reminds me of the case of Peter Scully. This is the most horrifying and disturbing child abuse case I've ever read about. I don't suggest learning about it, but if you must, I'd start with the 60 Minutes episode dedicated to his sick criminal empire.

In a nutshell, the Philippine-based Aussie would lure kids in, tie them up, and carry out painfully horrific things to them while filming it all. The child would then be killed on camera. Then, he'd sell the footage online as a pay-per-view subscription to sick buyers. Thankfully, Scully is now in jail, but I'm just as concerned about the hundreds of thousands of people - mostly from the US, UK, Australia, and Europe - buying these horrifying videos.

These people not only line the pockets of sadistic abusers but also view the footage for their own sick pleasure. They deserve to be traced, exposed, and made to face justice for their actions in propelling this sort of crime.

I feel exactly the same about the buyers of Dutroux's tapes.

As the months rolled by, the rapist wanted to acquire more victims. He'd also rounded up a small collective of accomplices: Michel Lelièvre and Bernard Weinstein would complete his sick crew. In the autumn of '95, Dutroux and Lelièvre abducted two girls from a train station. An Marchal, 17, and Eefje Lambrecks, 19, were brought back to Dutroux's property, but there was no room for them in the small cellar.

Instead, they were relegated to one of the bedrooms in the main portion of the house. They were tied to the bed, bound at their arms and legs. Yet again, horrific and repeated bouts of torture took place, all on camera. The daily routine of horror was constant for the girls, a seemingly never-ending nightmare they'd do anything to escape from. After a month of unbearable abuse, Dutroux and accomplice Bernard Weinstein transported the girls from the house of horror to one of Weinstein's homes.

It was here they terrifyingly met their end. Dutroux wouldn't offer any mercy by giving the teenagers a quick death. He wanted to make it as petrifying as possible. A slow death, where the victims knew their end was imminent.

He buried them alive.

Shortly thereafter, Weinstein stole a vehicle with another man and found himself in trouble with the law over this crime. Weinstein's name had been given to police over the theft, and he was a wanted man. This filled Dutroux with fear; his accomplice knew about all the horrific things he'd done, and a brush with the law may cause him to confess everything he knew. Dutroux didn't want to take this chance and killed him. Not before torturing him, though; he clamped the man's genitals to ensure maximum agony. Then, he buried him alive, leaving the body underneath one of his properties.

Toward the end of 1995, Dutroux was arrested on suspicion of car theft. He was behind bars for four months after being found guilty, leaving Julie Lejeune and Melissa Russo in their dank cellar alone. Dutroux was the one who brought them food and water. With him gone, the only other person who could do that job was Michelle Martin, the woman living right above them. Her partner had been sent away for a quarter of the year, and the girls would die if she didn't see to them.

Michelle didn't go down to the cellar once. She didn't consider giving them a glass of water and some sustenance, let alone setting them free. She merely ignored their existence. Acted like they weren't there.

Frustratingly, after Dutroux's arrest for the car theft, the police did a search of his home. The two girls were right there on the property, but the police didn't search hard enough to find them. Alongside the police, a locksmith was sent, just in case they found a secret area that Dutroux had constructed. The locksmith distinctly heard screams. He paused for a moment to make sure it wasn't in his head, and he was right - screams were coming from somewhere in the house.

He told the police, who advised him the screams were coming from the children who were playing in the street. The screams were of the terrified girls in the cold, dark cellar mere feet away from help.

Help would never come. The eight-year-olds would starve to death.

While searching the house, police picked up some videotapes scattered on the floor. These homemade tapes made their way into the police station - but nobody would watch them. If they just took the time to push the tape into the VCR, they'd be met with some sickening footage, but the girls would likely have been saved.

Dutroux was back on the streets by March 1996. Upon his return, he discovered the two girls were dead and buried them at one of his properties. It would take the serial sex offender just two months to find a new girl to occupy the cellar.

On May 28, 1996, 12-year-old Sabine Darden was making her way to school. A stroke of utter misfortune saw her catch Dutroux's eye. She'd never make it to school but instead ended up in the dungeon. His abuse of her was much the same as it was with every girl prior, although this time, he'd amp up his emotional abuse. He liked to feel dominant in every way, and it gave him a thrill to toy with his young victim. So, under the guise of doing something kind for the girl, he told Sabine to write to her family, and he'd make sure they got the letters. They never did. Dutroux would read them with great pleasure and use the information within them to manipulate the child.

In her heartbreaking letters, she told her mother she didn't think she'd ever see her again. She explained she didn't know where she was, but it was a "room of agony."

After almost three months of just evil Dutroux for company, Sabine was shocked to find another teenage girl thrown in the cellar alongside her. Terrified 14-year-old Laetitia Delhez stood shaking as Dutroux prompted Sabine to look at the girl. He brought the new girl in to keep his current abductee company, he said.

Little did Dutroux know when he took Laetitia from the street in broad daylight, someone saw him do it. In fact, the quick-thinking witness jotted down the first half of his number plate and got a thorough look at the make and model of the van that drove off with the teen. Dutroux had gotten over-confident, and it looked like it could be his downfall.

The police were informed about the kidnapping, and a hunt for the van ensued. A match was established, and it brought investors right to Marc Dutroux. The same day Laetitia was taken, authorities raided seven properties in Dutroux's name. As they did, they arrested the suspect, along with his wife Michelle and his accomplice Michel Lelièvre.

Dutroux wouldn't make things easy for the investigators. In fact, it seemed he got a kick from spinning different stories, contradicting himself, and throwing in red herrings. Hours passed, and police were getting nowhere with the criminal.

Meanwhile, one of Dutroux's neighbors came to authorities to tell them he'd witnessed Dutroux and Lelièvre transporting a female covered in a blanket from the house. Still, Dutroux would remain elusive and difficult when presented with this information. Hours turned into days, and it seemed the suspect wasn't waning from the constant interrogation. In fact, it seemed he was basking in it.

Eventually, though, it had to come to an end. Perhaps Dutroux believed there was no way out, that there was too much evidence for him to talk his way out of it. Or, maybe he just got bored. Either way, after days of making the police run in circles, he said he'd tell them where the girls were: they were where they'd been looking this whole time. He guided them to the dungeon, and thankfully, Sabine and Laetitia were still alive.

Distressed, traumatized, and starving, but they were alive. Footage of them being walked from Dutroux's dungeon is available online, and you can see the horror and disbelief in the girls' eyes. It's like they didn't think it was really happening and that they were in a dream they were surely going to wake up from.

The police knew this wasn't the extent of Dutroux's offending. Julie Lejeune and Melissa Russo were still missing from the year prior, and Dutroux was the main suspect. Again, the man proved to be difficult, switching from glib to cocky to playing dumb, all within the same sentence. Investigators just couldn't get him to be honest until he eventually agreed to give them what they wanted. It took two days of intense questioning for police to get this far. Dutroux gave them the address for his property in Marcinelle, telling investigators they'd find the girls there. He didn't mention they were dead. It seems Dutroux was having plenty of fun as he toyed with law enforcement.

Police raced to the property, scouring the area, hoping to rescue the two children. They would find the children wrapped in trash bags buried in the garden. They were a year too late. Dutroux would insist he wasn't guilty of killing the girls, blaming his partner Michelle for not feeding them in his absence. While, technically, this was true, he couldn't abolish all blame. After all, he was the one who'd locked them in there.

Alongside the macabre discovery of the girls was the uncovering of Bernard Weinstein's decomposing body.

Dutroux decided to throw another grenade by admitting to killing An Marchal and Eefje Lambrecks, guiding police to their bodies. It was clear both had been tortured. Forensic testing revealed they'd been raped.

The evidence was sprawling and complex. Once the public got wind of the crimes, they were appalled at the way police handled - or rather, mishandled - the case. Snippets of information trickled to the public, such as Dutroux's mother's letter to police the year before his arrest, telling them he was holding girls hostage at his property. Nothing was done with this information, despite Dutroux being a suspect in Julie Lejeune and Melissa Russo's disappearance.

Police visited Dutroux's house twice while the girls were being held there. They'd also taken tapes of his recording of abuse and not bothered to watch it. A plethora of DNA was found in the dungeon - a judge ruled this shouldn't be tested. There was a feeling law enforcement was dispassionate about the crimes of Dutroux and allowed him to get away with his vile crimes because of this.

Finally, just over seven years after his arrest, Dutroux was sent to trial. On March 1, 2001, he, Michelle, and their accomplice, Michel Lelièvre, faced a combined number of 235 charges. The trio were found guilty on all charges brought to them. The Belgian public wanted nothing less than the death penalty. There'd been marches, protests, and outcry over the sick spate of crimes, and it felt as though death for all involved would be the only way to satisfy the public's need for justice.

However, the death penalty was revoked in Belgium in 1996. Sentencing took place on June 22, 2004. Dutroux got life imprisonment, his wife was handed 30 years, and their accomplice Lelièvre was given 25 years.

Though the criminals were behind bars, there were many unanswered questions, which wasn't helped by Dutroux and his voicing of some new claims. He insisted he was a low-tier member of a pedophile group and even named the person he was working for: Michel Nihoul.

Dutroux wasn't exactly known for his truth-telling ability. But, there may be some truth in what he was confessing to. Nihoul was a wealthy, well-connected businessman known to be a regular at sex parties. Dutroux claimed he acquired girls for the man, an accusation Nihoul's lawyer scoffed at. Still, when a reporter covering the case tried to speak with Nihoul and get his version of events, he warned her, "I am the monster of Belgium." If this wasn't chilling enough, he grabbed her forcefully and pulled her onto his lap, causing the woman to cry for help.

Nihoul was never charged with any involvement in the case.

Dutroux said he kept the girls in his specially-made dungeon to keep them safe from the pedophiles. Instead of handing them over, as his job required, he began keeping them to "save them." I'm not sure torturing and raping them would ever be considered saving them, but Dutroux had already proved he had a warped view of reality. He went on to claim that he killed Bernard Weinstein only as an act of revenge for allowing girls to die.

This version of events was contradicted by his wife Michelle's take on the whole sickening story. She said her husband had wanted to abduct girls since the mid-80s and tried to convince Michelle this was a good thing. If he had "affairs," as he put it, he'd offer her more in the way of attention and affection.

Michelle served 16 years of her sentence and is now a free woman.

Today, Dutroux insists he's no longer dangerous. He has applied numerous times to be paroled, requesting to be put on house arrest and wear an ankle tag.

With crimes as depraved and despicable as Marc Dutroux's, I don't think you could ever consider him a low risk to the public. In order to secure early release, three separate psychiatrists have to sign him off as being unlikely to reoffend. Dutroux has proven he can fool psychiatrists in the past; let's hope history doesn't repeat itself.

Hotel Of Horror

I've mentioned this before, but tales of cannibalism really make me shudder. The idea that a human can consume another fills me with a feeling of sickness. When I first read about this story years ago, it made me feel queasy, to say the least. However, when more details of the gory crime came to light, it wasn't as it seemed.

Mandy Miles was a hotel owner in Caerphilly, a relatively quiet town in Wales. Her hotel could have been described as a hybrid between a budget hotel and a hostel. Many of the people who resided here were long-term residents with a troubled background. Some of them had been released from prison and stayed at the hotel until permanent accommodation came up. One of those people was 34-year-old Matthew Williams.

Williams was a violent man. He was known to be abusive in his relationships, and even those close to Williams weren't always sure what frame of mind the man might be in. He was in and out of jail for violent offenses and despite multiple incarcerations, never seemed to repent for his crimes. Certainly, there was never any remorse for his victims.

In 2013, Williams was in jail for beating an ex-girlfriend. He got a five-and-a-half-year term, although he didn't use this time to rethink his harmful behavior. Instead, the man's violent temper simmered beneath the surface, which was exhibited in the letters he wrote while behind bars.

He even had the brazenness to write to the woman he'd beaten. There was no apology, no asking for forgiveness, and absolutely zero repentance. In fact, there were more threats of violence; the very crime that landed him in jail. He warned that if the woman didn't get back together with Williams when he was released, he'd beat her again. In the same letter, he professed his love to her. It's clear the man was unhinged, and it was thought he suffered from schizophrenia since he told psychiatrists he heard voices and suffered hallucinations.

In these letters, he also threatened the officers who'd arrested him, threatening to kill them upon his release. Dark drawings accompanied his messages of vengeance, alongside the words, "snitches get stitches."

While in jail, the offender was put on report half a dozen times, some of which were due to violent behavior. One of those times was because of the disturbing letters he was sending. Officers confronted the man about the threats contained in the letters and requested an interview with him. Williams agreed, but when it came time to meet with officers, he wouldn't come out of his cell.

His probation report deemed him unfit for release, citing his violent behavior, lack of compliance, the threats he was sending while incarcerated, and his lack of motivation to better himself.

Still, Matthews was released in October 2014, and just days later, would kill Cerys Yemm in the hotel he was staying at.

Cerys was a popular 22-year-old from Oakdale, a village in Caerphilly. She had an on-off relationship with a man her mother described as "controlling." At one point, Cerys took shelter in a women's refuge but ended up returning back to her partner, which is sadly often the case for abused women.

Her boyfriend was in and out of jail over the course of the relationship, and it was while he was incarcerated he met Matthew Williams. Cerys promised her boyfriend she'd wait for him and was planning a future with him when he was released.

Cerys had more freedom with her partner in jail. She was able to enjoy nights out, and this is how she met and befriended Matthew Williams. Williams bought the young woman a drink and asked her to join him back to the hotel, an invite she accepted. She told her boyfriend that she met him but was warned to stay away from him. He was bad news, a dangerous man, her boyfriend told her.

Still, Cerys kept in touch with Williams and, by all accounts, was acting like she was in a relationship with the man. On November 5, she spent the entire day with him and one of his friends. The trio sat in his hotel room, drinking beer and getting high. Although things got rowdy, the group had to be quiet - guests were forbidden. He'd snuck his friends in successfully, and if they were kicked out, their day of drunkenness would be halted to a stop. The hours rolled by, and Williams' friend decided it was time he went home.

Cerys was due home that night, and her mother was getting worried as the night drew to a close and her daughter was nowhere to be seen.

She couldn't, in her worst nightmares, imagine what was happening to her daughter.

At some point, Williams had turned from charming to violent. It could have been due to his mental health problems, but then again, the plethora of drugs in his system can't have helped his mental struggles.

Hotel owner Mandy Miles was awoken by blood-curdling screams coming from Williams' room. She raced to his room and upon opening the door, was met with a sickening sight: Matthews was hunched over his victim, blood covering his face, his eyes black. The woman on the floor was lifeless, her left eye missing, her face crimson red with blood. In shock, Mandy asked Williams what he was doing to the girl. "That's no girl," he replied, continuing his attack.

Realizing the danger she was in, Mandy shut the room door, holding on to the handle from the outside to keep the killer locked in. With her other hand, she dialed 999. "There's a lad in room seven - he's actually eating her," she told the call handler. When police arrived, they tried to calm the man down but were unsuccessful. They tased him four times, resulting in Williams suffering a heart attack. He wouldn't recover from this, which is still a more humane way to go than he offered his victim.

Cerys had 89 separate injuries on her small frame. She'd been hit in the head with a blunt object, stabbed in the face with an unknown sharp object, and had numerous bite marks. He'd ripped an eye from his victim. The majority of the damage was inflicted on Cerys' face and head. Her mouth, nose, and eyes were all stabbed at with the weapon, resulting in her facial arteries being cut. This caused the woman to lose copious amounts of blood in a very short space of time. The sharp object also punctured her jugular vein, further compounding the amount of blood she was losing.

Her cause of death was blood loss.

Mandy had told police she thought Williams had used a screwdriver in his attack, although this wasn't retrieved from the crime scene. She also told them the killer was eating his victim, but a post-mortem exam found the woman hadn't been eaten. Certainly, Williams hadn't swallowed any of her flesh. However, Williams had used his mouth as a weapon, and ripping at her tissue with his teeth may not count as cannibalism, but is an act of extreme violence that certainly makes me feel queasy.

The crime sickened the town of Caerphilly, and the rumors of cannibalism were circulating. As people learned of the crime, they also began asking questions. The main one being, why was Matthew Williams released to kill?

It's not like the red flags weren't abundant.

Williams was a troubled child, difficult to control, and forever in trouble at school. He began using drugs at just 11 years old, and his violent temper saw him sent to a young offenders institute by age 15.

Over the course of his 34 years, Williams racked up 78 offenses, most of them violent. He was sent to youth justice institutions 41 times before he turned 18. He'd been to jail 14 times prior to his death.

While incarcerated, he was diagnosed with schizophrenia. However, this would be disputed after his death, with his forensic psychiatrist saying the man "clearly didn't have schizophrenia." She suggested that his drug use was the most likely culprit for his hallucinations and hearing voices. Indeed, in the two weeks from his prison release and his murder of Cerys, he'd had drugs every single day, particularly amphetamine.

Williams was initially prescribed antipsychotic medication, but this was stopped when he wasn't showing any signs of needing it. He was intermittent with his taking of the medication anyway, often refusing to take it. The man visited his GP just before he carried out the attack on Cerys, and the notes suggest that Williams appeared to be doing well.

Most of Williams' schizophrenia symptoms tied in with the side-effect of drug usage. His complaints of hearing voices, seeing things that weren't there, and losing the ability to communicate were all also side effects of amphetamines, a drug he took regularly.

It's been suggested that on the night of the murder, Williams encountered "agitated delirium." When officers arrived, he showed no response to pain, no response to verbal commands, and was growling. It took a number of officers to restrain the man, with one holding his arms, another holding his feet, and another trying to restrain him via his torso. Still, he exhibited unusual strength and fought all three officers off him. This is also a side effect of amphetamines.

While his mental health diagnosis may have been in question, his love of drugs and use of violence were not. When the two were combined, the results were often catastrophic. Williams was known to be a risk, especially to women. The owner of the hotel he was housed in wasn't given his background information due to data protection, so she had no clue what kind of criminal she was housing.

Matthew Williams was released from jail with no supervision, no curfew, no mental health referral, and no concrete mental health diagnosis. He shouldn't have been on the streets; this much was agreed within the Caerphilly community. Why he was, despite being deemed a risk, is a question still unanswered.

Heists And Homicide

A single-story house is somewhere between 10 to 15 feet in height. That's about seventeen bricks, give or take. It's also roughly the same height as Gary Evans' rap sheet if you printed it out and taped it all together. This career criminal and confessed serial killer was truly one heinous individual whose story could be akin to that of a villain in an action movie.

Gary Evans was born in 1954 in Troy, New York. Sadly, as is the case with many children who go on to become criminals, Gary was abused by his parents. Certainly, children who aren't abused can (and do) become killers, just like in the case of Joanna Dennehy. But, frequently, murderers endured a traumatic upbringing, which was the case for Gary. He endured beatings, humiliating emotional abuse, and witnessed abuse between his parents.

The boy would also claim his father raped him when he was just eight years old, a truly sickening act if true, although this alleged assault has never been proven. It might be worth mentioning here that although Gary would grow up to be a serial criminal and murderer, he wasn't known for outlandish lies or telling tall tales.

The couple divorced when Gary was 14, but the damage had been done by then.

He was left in the care of his mother, who continued mistreating the child. She'd encourage him to go steal, and the young boy got an eye for the luxurious and expensive at a young age. Soon, he was stealing jewelry. This would be the start of a lifelong career as a thief.

It didn't stop there for the young boy. His antisocial behavior turned into violence, and he began killing animals. Often, these were his neighbors' pets, but young Gary didn't care. He clearly showed signs of having an antisocial personality disorder, but this would never be something the child would be offered help for. As we now know, those who go on to kill often start by harming animals. It's a huge red flag, a twisted act that may as well cause the killer to hold up a sign saying, "humans are next." Often, they are, and this was certainly the case for Gary Evans.

At the age of 16, the youth was sent to juvenile detention after getting caught stealing. He'd been thieving from a young age, so for it to have taken around ten years for the serial looter to be captured is surprising. But, then again, as you'll discover, Gary had an innate ability to carry out robberies successfully. He treated it like an art; the planning, the preparation, and the ability to execute the scheme smoothly gave him a misguided sense of purpose.

By the time he came out of detention the following year, his mother had married and divorced a number of different men. Her alcoholism had escalated, which was perhaps a big factor in her unstable romantic relationships. It was during this time his mother also came out as gay, which was maybe the root reason for her need to drink: she'd been suppressing her true desires for years.

Still, Gary's rocky relationship with his mother didn't seem to improve. If anything, their bickering and arguing only escalated, so as he entered his 20s, he moved out of the family home and entered a brief life of vagrancy. Still, if there was anything Gary was capable of, it was being self-sufficient. However, his method of doing this always saw him leaving a trail of chaos in his wake. From robbing drug dealers to looting random homes, the young man made sure he had what he needed to survive. For Gary, stealing wasn't just a means of living; it seems like it became his reason to live.

In cases like this, I always wonder how different things could have been if the criminal had placed their abilities and talents in the right direction. Gary was methodical, a good planner, and thought outside the box. He was clever, creative, and had a high-risk appetite. He'd have been an asset in a number of careers or perhaps been more suited to building a successful business of his own. Instead, Gary chose to channel his attributes into criminal (and eventually murderous) endeavors.

After his short stint on the streets, Gary reconnected with some childhood friends, Michael Falco and Timothy Rysedorph. The trio ended up living together, and their apartment was a melting pot of criminal minds. Each of the young men was a thief, and together, they became partners in crime. Gary took his role in the group seriously and began taking a keen interest in jewelry and antiques, learning as much about them as possible.

With this newfound wealth of knowledge, the thief would use his expertise to get in front of professional art dealers and get inside their studios. While he was doing so, along with Michael and Timothy, he'd scope the premises, figuring out the best way to break in and steal the high-value goods. The trio would pull off robberies straight out of heist movies, figuring out how to deactivate antique shops' alarm systems, breaking in via tunneling through the walls, and making off with the goods.

As good as he was, Gary couldn't avoid jail time. He was in and out for petty thefts in the late 70s and early 80s and was treated as an inmate who was an escape risk. This was warranted - in June 1980, he managed to jump the wall and escape prison. It was a dramatic affair, which ended when he ran into the Troy Public Library and climbed from a window, leaving him teetering on the ledge. Spectators gathered to look up at the criminal on the run as police cars surrounded the library. The public began to cheer and yell as the criminal entertained them, only for him to be captured by the police. It was straight back to jail for Gary, who spent his time devising better escape plans.

Over the next few years, he was in and out of prison. Each time he was released, he resumed his antique thievery, with no amount of jail time enough of a deterrent to stop him. He and his two buddies would scope out dealers to rob and would execute the plan together, mostly getting away with it.

However, the relationship with his partner Timothy soured, and by 1985, the pair were no longer talking. It was just Gary and Michael carrying out the heists, and their first job as a duo saw them rake in a profit of $15,000. Today, that would be around $55,000, not a sum to be sniffed at. Certainly, the pair thought it was worth the possibility of going to jail.

Instead of laying low, Gary couldn't help but continue his criminal activities, and his next crime would see him again in trouble with the law. He was able to wangle his way out of it, though. The charge was for selling a stolen car, but after Gary admitted his crime and promised to get a proper job, he was allowed to walk free.

Gary didn't get a real job. In fact, his rap sheet was only going to get longer.

By the end of July 1985, he'd committed his first murder. It wasn't for any kind of gain or to evade capture from a robbery. It was the cold-blooded murder of his accomplice, Micahel Falco. Timothy had come back on the scene, and he didn't have good things to say about Michael. He confided in Gary that their business partner had been sneakily selling the stolen goods and pocketing the profit for himself. This caused Gary to seek vengeance and saw him build his own silencer to attach to his pistol in preparation for the killing. He'd use this weapon to end his double-crossing partner's life.

In reality, his partner hadn't double-crossed him. Not Michael, anyway - Timothy had been the one selling their goods for his own gain.

Still, Gary didn't know this and even enlisted the help of Timothy to dispose of Michael's body. Gary dismembered his former friend before Timothy took the bloody body parts and hid them in a sleeping bag. He transferred the body all the way from Troy to Florida, a 20-hour drive. Gary's sister lived here, and the pair used her backyard to bury the limbs, head, and torso of Michael Falco.

The criminal duo spent nearly two months in Palm Beach soaking up the rays. They couldn't stay in paradise forever, though, and they had business in Troy to deal with. Upon their return, Gary was arrested and handed a prison term for violating his parole conditions for the car theft. Again, it would be the start of an on-off relationship with prison.

In the spring of 1988, Gary was once again free. He would meet Damien Cuomo, a young man who was a career criminal and, just like Gary, specialized in theft. The two would join forces and carry out many sophisticated robberies. However, the pair didn't have a long run together; they had a year of crime before the police caught up with them. When authorities arrested them, they were armed with stun guns, radio scanners and even ski masks. These are all items you'd imagine every thief would own, and you'd think these items alone would be incriminating enough to send Gary back to jail. Especially considering his previous convictions for theft.

However, he and Damien were set free since the evidence was circumstantial. In Gary's case, he was released to kill again.

If he'd been handed yet another jail term, perhaps he wouldn't have killed 63-year-old Douglas Berry, a vintage shop owner. After coldly shooting the man, he and Damien looted the place and made off with a hefty amount of antique goods. It's unclear as to why Douglas had to die, but Gary's second murder was executed just as carefully as his first. There was no evidence left behind, nothing to tie him to the crime, and no leads for the police to follow.

Towards the end of 1989, Damien began to suffer from mental health problems. He was depressed, and his shift in mood was noticed by Gary, who wasn't sympathetic to his partner's suffering. In fact, his answer to his former friend's low mood was to kill him. Gary was worried that 28-year-old Damien's depression would cause him to tell the police what the criminals had been up to, notably that Gary had killed a man. After another killing, Gary returned to Florida but quickly moved to California.

Armed robber, murderer, and now, a sexual pest.

While in California, Gary bumped into a woman he'd known for years. She rejected his advances, which caused him to verbally abuse her, threatening her for daring to say no to him. This resulted in Gary's arrest, but no criminal charges were given since he agreed to leave California. It was back to Troy for the criminal. It was now autumn 1991, around two years since his last kill. His return to New York saw the serial killer add another number to his ever-increasing tally of victims.

Yet again, he targeted a vintage shop owner, a man in his 30s called Gregory Jouben. Where before, Gary would meticulously plan his heists, covertly taking the goods without killing anybody, it seems he got lazy: it was easier to kill people than it was to use his sneaky wiles to loot the antiques. He made $60,000 for this robbery, which would work out around $135,000 today.

Meanwhile, Gary was consoling Damien Cuomo's girlfriend. He'd told her that Damien had left her and their young daughter and fled the area, suggesting he didn't think he'd be coming back. Eventually, the pair embarked on a romantic relationship, with Gary often caring for Damien's little girl.

The persistent killing appeared to take its toll on Gary, however. Unusually for a criminal, he decided the murder of Gregory Jouben was his last. He was going to go clean. He'd get a real job. Maybe start a family. Live a normal life. Before he did, though, he carried out one last criminal act. He reasoned that he needed a safety net of cash and stole a 1,000-pound marble tombstone from the cemetery. He sold it, pocketed the money, and kept his promise to himself: he did begin to live a crime-free life.

Well, mostly. Sometimes he just couldn't help himself. It was like an urge he had to keep in check at all times. His desire to thieve and hustle was occasionally overwhelming. He would steal something small or commit a petty crime just to fulfill those impulses.

Three years after he stole the marble headstone, he was arrested for it. Those three years of (mostly) clean living hadn't done him any favors. Karma didn't care. He was jailed for the theft.

Upon his release, he relinquished his previous promise to himself. He began living a life of crime yet again. He became a survivalist and forfeited his apartment in favor of a tent. One of his heists during this time was of a valuable book, and it took him over a year to find a buyer. In his quest to offload this book, one of the potential buyers contacted the police, who quickly arrested the serial criminal.

The police were sick of the persistent thief darkening their doorstep. Gary was told he was looking at a long time behind bars for his continuous criminal activity - possibly life. This threat prompted the culprit to admit the book's location and hand it back unscathed. He was only given two years in jail since he returned the goods and never gained anything from the theft.

He remained behind bars until the summer of 1996, which saw him rescind his survivalist lifestyle and move back in with his old heist partner, Timothy Rysedorph. They'd both spent the past few years honing their skills, so when they reunited, they began carrying out highly sophisticated robberies. They left no evidence to avoid being recognized and even rented a dedicated storage unit for their dirty goods.

Gary couldn't shake the paranoia he felt about Timothy knowing he shot and killed Michael Falco all those years ago. Despite the pair carrying out crime after crime together, Gary began to feel uneasy. He was sure Timothy would hand him over to the police, and if they were caught, his partner could use this information as leverage with the police. It was decided - Timothy had to die. After shooting his partner to death, just like he did with Michael, he cut the body up and buried it in a desolate wooded area.

Whenever he carried out a murder, Gary tended to feel the need to escape New York. It might have been a fear of being arrested, feelings of guilt, or trying to distance himself from the bad things he'd done, but fleeing was always the reaction Gary had. This was against his probation, and it wasn't long before police figured Gary had skipped town yet again.

Timothy had a wife and son. When the man never returned home, the police were called, resulting in a manhunt for the missing father. Authorities were suspicious of Gary Evans and were trying to track him down as a person of interest. Their search led them to Damien Cuomo's girlfriend, who guided the police to Gary.

At this point, there was no evidence to suggest Gary was a murderer. The police didn't have any evidence to charge him with any murder. They strongly suspected he was involved in Timothy's disappearance, but they had no clue about the murders Gary had carried out over the years. He executed these killings so meticulously that he'd likely never have been caught if he never told anybody.

However, as soon as the police found him, he admitted everything. He told investigators where all the bodies were buried and confessed to everything he'd ever done. The police had captured a serial killer they had no idea was on the loose.

In August 1998, Gary Evans was due to be charged with the murders he'd confessed to. While being transported to court, the vehicle passed the Menands Bridge. Prior to this, Gary had removed a key he'd hidden up his nose to free himself from his handcuffs and ankle chains. He smashed the window and jumped out of the vehicle as it moved, running as fast as he could as the police chased him. Officers quickly caught up with the escapee, but they didn't bank on Gary having other plans: he'd been planning this escape for a while. He did not intend to serve life in jail or be sentenced to death. Well, he knew death was imminent, but it would be at his own hands. He couldn't face a life of confinement. He found himself towering over the Hudson River before looking down and leaping to his death.

Gary had let his longtime lawyer know he planned on killing himself, although he'd perhaps never taken his client seriously. He'd mentioned it to him years ago, stating that he'd be unable to deal with a lifetime in jail. Prior to jumping to his death, while planning his final act, he sent a letter to one of the investigators, expressing regret over his life choices.

Those close to Gary also said that should have been given the death sentence, this would have troubled him deeply. Not because it meant a premature death but because of the injection used to kill him: Gary was staunchly against drug taking, particularly drugs via injection. Despite his proclivity for murder and mayhem, the criminal was otherwise pretty straight-laced: he didn't drink, smoke, or eat meat.

This criminal clearly had a complex mind with conflicting worldviews and offered a glimmer of remorse about the atrocities he'd carried out, unlike most serial killers.

Merciless Mass Murderer

The 60s, 70s, and 80s are all decades where serial killers seemed to thrive. They hosted the appalling crimes of Ted Bundy, Jeffery Dahmer, The Zodiac Killer, Fred West, and Ed Kemper, to name but a few. There's a lesser-known killer among those ranks, but don't let his relatively undiscussed acts fool you: his crimes were abysmal. He preyed on teen boys and abused them in horrific ways before ending their short lives, all for his own twisted pleasure.

Dean Corll was born on Christmas Eve, 1939, in Indiana. His mother coddled him, whereas his father was the complete opposite. The boy clung to his mother and grew detached from his stern father. The parents rarely got along, often arguing in front of the child. In 1941, the quarreling managed to cease enough for Mary Corll to become pregnant again, and in 1942, The Corll family introduced another little boy named Stanley. Aside from his brother, Dean didn't bother too much with other kids.

It wasn't that the boy was antisocial - far from it - he was just shy and introverted. He would express concern for his fellow schoolmates and would become distressed if other children hurt themselves. In all, Dean was an empathetic, emotionally intelligent child. Sadly, this empathy wouldn't follow him to adulthood.

The Corll parents eventually divorced, although a few reconciliations and break-ups followed, denting the sensitive boy's need for stability. The fiery couple would end up going their separate ways permanently when Mary married a man named Jake West, who would become the Corll boys' stepfather. Jake and Mary went on to have a child together, and the blended family eventually settled in Vidor, Texas, in the 50s.

Here, Jake became self-employed, opening a candy factory. It was an ideal place for a teen boy to work, packaging the candy and overseeing the candy-making machines. Dean and his brother excelled at their roles in their stepdad's factory and spent evenings and weekends here making the sweet treats while Jake would take the product out on the road and sell it to various establishments. It was the picture-perfect family business.

Despite spending plenty, if not all, of his free time at the factory, Dean's school grades didn't falter. He was an above-average achiever with a solid work ethic. The only thing he didn't excel at was making friends. He hit his late teens and hadn't found someone to befriend, much less found a group of friends. He would, on occasion, ask a girl out on a date, but it never went too far. Dean wasn't really interested in girls or dating. Especially girls; he only dated them to fit in. Dean was harboring some dark, disturbing desires, none involving females. They involved young boys.

Dean graduated in 1958, coinciding with the family pulling stakes to Houston, Texas. The candy had proved to be most successful in Houston, with the majority of buyers residing there. It just made business sense for the family, and they branched out by opening their own candy store in the city. However, Dean was sent back to Indiana shortly after to take care of his frail grandmother. She was a widow, and Dean took care of her well. He'd humor her, help her around the house, and offer the older woman some much-needed company.

While in his home state, he began dating a girl. It's unclear if he did this to appease his grandmother or if he took a genuine interest in the young woman. Still, Dean didn't see a future with his love interest, although she had different ideas. In order to secure a commitment from her boyfriend, she asked Dean to marry her. He declined, the relationship ended, and the young woman's heart was broken.

Dean didn't have to worry too much about bumping into his ex around town since he quickly moved back to Houston to be with his mother. However, upon his reuniting with his family, he found it in a state of disarray. His mother and stepfather were constantly arguing. The hostile environment he returned to wouldn't last too long since the couple divorced in 1963.

Mary would take her decade of experience working in the candy business and open up her own establishment: The Corll Candy Company. Reliable, hardworking Dean was handed the vice-president role and played a key part in hiring and training new staff. The staff Dean sought were teenage boys. Shortly after the new business was up and running, one of the boys working in the store complained to Mary that her son had made unwanted sexual advances toward him.

Mary didn't speak to Dean or consider the teenage boy's side. In response to his allegations, Mary fired the young worker. In hindsight, Mary saved the teenager from the possibility of more undesired sexual passes, an unintentional positive from unfairly sacking the boy who was asking for help.

By the time 1964 rolled around, Dean had been drafted into the Army and sent to Louisiana for a lengthy training regime. While here, Dean was able to explore his homosexual desires, and the ten months he was away saw him confirm what he already knew: he was gay. Despite his time in the Army offering him an outlet to explore his sexuality, he hated being away from home.

To get back to Houston, he applied for a hardship discharge, stating his mother needed him back home to run the family business. This was granted his request, and he was given an honorable discharge on June 11, 1965.

Life returned to normal for Dean. He ran the candy store, made a healthy amount of money, and, on the outside, looked like he was carving a successful life for himself. He employed solely teen boys to work in his store, which was relocated to reside in front of an elementary school. Dean would frequently hand out free candy to the kids as they left school, earning him the moniker "candy man" among the teens who recognized him.

To retain an atmosphere where teen boys would want to work, Dean bought a pool table for the back room of the Corll Candy Company. This area would house the young workers and their friends, becoming a place to hang out for the local teenage boys.

On the inside, though, Dean was unhappy. He was living a lie, unable to meet a partner he was interested in, and the candy store takings began to wane. Eventually, he had no choice but to close the company.

Dean was bright, articulate, and intelligent, so it didn't take him long to find another job. He got a well-paying position at the Houston Lighting and Power Company and found himself with more time to hang out with someone he'd recently befriended at his pool table: a 12-year-old boy called David Brooks.

By this point, Dean was around 30-years-old. At the time, perhaps people thought Dean was a big-brother type figure for David or offering some fatherly company for the boy. The two would often take long drives together, and Dean would make sure the boy wasn't short of cash for anything he needed.

It wasn't long before Dean would encourage the boy to engage in sexual acts. The boy would receive money for carrying out illicit and illegal acts on the older man. Things were about to get much more depraved for the perverted man, though. He'd go from twisted sexual abuse to the full-on torture, rape, and eventual murders of at least 28 boys.

His first victim was an 18-year-old called Jeffrey Konen. Dean was 31 years old and wasn't getting enough of a thrill from the abuse of young boys - he wanted to exercise complete control over his victims. He wanted to act out his dark, depraved thoughts and not have to worry about being outed for them.

Jeffery was hitchhiking to Houston when Dean spotted him thumbing around a residential area by himself. Spotting an opportunity, Dean pulled up beside the teenager and asked where he was going. "I'm trying to get to my parent's home. It's not too far," Jeffery said. Dean invited the hitchhiker to get in, knowing full well he'd never make it to his parents. Instead, the young man was taken to Dean's apartment and subjected to unimaginable torture and abuse. He was raped, beaten, and eventually strangled to death. In order to ensure the victim's death, Dean callously forced an old rag into the man's mouth.

After killing Jeffery, Dean covered the corpse in lime, bound it in a plastic covering, and buried it where no one would ever find it underneath a practically immovable boulder on High Island Beach. Dean was sure the body wouldn't be discovered. Unless, of course, his good friend David Brooks ever decided to tell the police where the body was.

Young David was quickly being exposed to more and more trauma at the hands of the man he looked up to like a father. As well as being sexually abused by Dean, David bore witness to the older man's newfound acts of kidnapping, torture, rape, and murder. Shortly after the murder of Jeffery, David walked into Dean's room, only to find two young boys tied up on torture boards. Dean was sexually abusing both of them.

This disturbed David. He raced out of the room, trying to process the horrors he'd walked in on. Two teens, tied up, bloodied, being violated horrifically by Dean. However, the older man bought his silence. Dean would buy him a new car in return for keeping his mouth shut. The killer came through with his promise, and teenage David was the first of all his peers to be driving around in a sports car.

This marked the beginning of a new relationship between the two. Dean suggested they come to an agreement that would benefit both of them. David would get $200 for every teen boy he brought back to Corll's residence. When David asked what would happen to the boys, Dean didn't hesitate. They'd meet the same fate as every other boy who'd entered his bedroom - they'd be killed.

Near Christmas 1970, David followed through with his part of the deal. He'd been in Houston Heights earlier that day and met 14-year-olds James Glass and Danny Yates. The pair of teens had no idea the evil that awaited them at Corll's residence. They were tied up on either side of his bed, facing opposite directions, and were brutally tortured. Some of the torture involved both boys being electrocuted, with Dean holding the electrical cords to abuse them at a whim. They were raped, beaten, and eventually killed by the sick killer when he'd had his fun. Dean got rid of the bodies by burying them underneath his boat shed.

David got his $400. For a young boy, this would have seemed like an unbelievable amount of money. Perhaps it was addictive, despite the depths he had to go in order to earn it.

Just a month after the murders of James and Danny, David helped Dean lure two more teen boys back to his house. Brothers Donald and Jerry Waldrop were making their way home from a friend's house when Dean and his young protégé rolled up beside them. The pair accepted a ride but would never make it home. Instead, they found themselves tied up in Dean's torture room.

The same sick acts were carried out on the terrified teens. They were abused in horrific ways before being disposed of underneath the boat shed.

The summer of 1971 saw Dean and David prowl the streets, seeking out young boys, either alone or in pairs. In a matter of a few months, they worked together to lure 15-year-old Randell Harvey, 13-year-old David Hilligiest, and 16-year-old Gregory Malley Winkle to Dean's home. Every boy suffered the same agonizing torture before their inevitable murder.

The thing about targeting teen boys is there were always worried parents who would never stop searching for their beloved children. However, it was the 70s, and runaways were common, so many of these missing children were dismissed as such. Still, it didn't stop those who cared about the boys from trying to figure out what happened to them. The friends of the missing teens would hand out posters seeking information about the whereabouts of their peers.

Elmer Wayne Henley was good friends with David Hilligiest. The pair had been friends as far back as they could remember, and Elmer wanted to help the Hilligiest family find the boy.

So, he took a bunch of the posters offering a reward for David's return and stuck them up around town. It wasn't like David to just take off, and Elmer knew this, but he still tried to console himself that his friend had run away to start a new life. Elmer was a good kid, a pleasant 15-year-old who'd always been a loyal friend. In the year to come, this would all change under the influence of Dean Corll.

In the meantime, Dean and his young accomplice were racking up the numbers. 17-year-old Ruben Watson Haney was abducted, tortured, sexually abused, and killed. Again, the victim ended up underneath the boat shed. Up until the winter of 1971, it's thought the pair managed to secure more unknown victims.

David Brooks was good friends with Elmer Henley. David was running out of acquaintances to lure back to Dean's house, and the $200 payments were drying up. So, he enticed his pal Elmer over to the torture house in anticipation of another lump sum payment. However, much to David's surprise, Dean didn't abuse Elmer. In fact, he had a proposition for him: $200 for any teen boy he could lure into his home. The exact same sick deal he'd struck with David.

When the boy asked what for, Dean didn't tell the truth, but his lie was just as chilling. He said he was high up in a slavery ring, an operation working out of Dallas, and he needed to acquire boys for his boss. The money, much like it did with David, reeled Elmer in. Not right away, though; it took a few months before the teen agreed to work for Dean.

It was Dean's lifestyle that really impressed Elmer. His home, car, and lifestyle all showed what surplus money could buy, and since Elmer's family was struggling financially, he had nothing in the way of luxuries. Not like Dean, who had all the amenities a young boy could dream of. It wasn't long before Elmer acquired his first catch and brought him to Dean's home.

Elmer didn't stick around to see the sickening acts of depravity carried out on the teen he'd lured to a cruel fate. For his second victim, though, he'd find out what kind of twisted things Corll was into.

Frank Aguirre was a friend of Elmer's. He was a few years older at 18, but the pair crossed paths frequently. Frank was working at a restaurant, and Elmer decided he and Dean should visit his workplace, offer him some beers, and see if he wanted to get high. Elmer knew the answer would be yes, and it would be an easy $200 for just a few minutes of work. Frank, excited to sip some cold beers after a long shift, readily got in Corll's vehicle and was taken to his house of horrors.

The three enjoyed a few beers and shared a joint before Dean turned violent, restraining Frank and cuffing his hands behind his back. Elmer was now privy to the real reason Dean wanted him to acquire young boys: for their systematic rape, torture, and murder. Still, the teen didn't run for the hills. He stayed and helped bury the body. Yet again, another young corpse was buried underneath the boat house.

Now Elmer was in on the true depravity of Dean's actions, and he and David began taking a more active role in the abuse. This part of the case I struggle to understand. Was it a shared trauma that caused the boys to begin abusing the victims they lured in for Dean? Had they been so desensitized by what they'd witnessed - boys, sometimes their friends - stripped of their clothing, tied by the hands and feet, and brutalized in the most horrific ways imaginable. It's hard to know for sure. Perhaps both boys had an inner penchant for cruelty that was brought out by their inappropriate relationship with Dean.

The three took their next victim in the spring of '72. A 17-year-old who was well-acquainted with David and Elmer. Mark Scott was brought to Dean's house willingly but soon changed his mind when the atmosphere soured. There was no way Dean was letting him out of the house alive, and there was no chance David and Elmer wanted to give up their combined $400 bounty.

Mark fought back valiantly. He even managed to pick up a knife and hold it before his three attackers, warning them he'd use it unless they set him free. That was until he saw Elmer in the corner of the room, pistol in hand, pointing straight toward him. All hope left his body. The will to fight for his life had gone. He'd been scuffling and fighting the three of his attackers for some time, and he was tired. Mark knew resistance was futile, so he fell to the floor. His only sliver of hope now was that he'd be set free once Dean was finished with him.

The teen was tied to the torture board, which had been used in multiple torture murders. It had been the dying place for many a teenage boy, a sick tool used by a sick man. After enduring horrendous abuse and multiple sexual assaults, Mark ended up underneath the boat house.

David and Elmer were ready to up their levels of sadism. The next attack saw the two boys partake in a much more involved way. After Dean had tortured and violated his next two victims - Billy Baulch and Johnny Delome - the boys entered the bedroom with their own twisted torture to inflict. Elmer forced Johnny to watch as he shot his friend point-blank in the head. This was the teenager's first solo kill. The pair then strangled Johnny to death, which would have been a truly terrifying and prolonged way to die. He was powerless to prevent the pair - people he'd considered friends before this - from killing him.

Dean was getting more confident with his criminal activities and began treating his accomplices as expendable. In a way, they were. Plenty of teens from low-income families would do anything for an extra $200. Dean, for his insatiable desire for dominance, decided to pit the teens against each other.

Elmer punched David to the ground, rendering him unconscious. He did so at the behest of Dean, who then dragged an incapacitated David to the plywood torture board. Here, he raped him. There's no doubt David knew what was coming - a world of unimaginable pain followed by him joining the rest of the teen boys buried under the boat house. But death never came. After being abused multiple times, David was set free from the board. You'd expect him to run far, far away from the twisted man, but he didn't. He stuck around and continued to procure boys for his abuser.

The summer of 1972 saw the three lure in 17-year-old Steven Sickman and 19-year-old Roy Bunton. Unimaginable cruelty was inflicted upon the pair before they were bundled into the bottom of the boat house. As summer drew to a close, David and Elmer were driving around Houston Heights in search of another boy. Despite Elmer attacking David, it seemed there was nothing anybody could do to deter him from being part of Dean's inner circle, and he happily stuck around.

The two boys, cruising in the car Dean had bought David, soon happened upon Wally Simoneaux and Richard Hembree. The pair were lured back to the house of horrors, only to be set upon by Dean and his young aides. Heartbreakingly, partway through being attacked, Wally managed to find the phone, dial his mother's home number, and when she answered, he yelled "Mama" down the phone. After the blood-curdling scream, the line was cut dead. This was the last anybody would hear of Wally, except, of course, the three individuals torturing him.

Elmer and David seemed to enjoy tormenting and goading the victims as they lay helpless on the torture board. The infliction of pain was carried out in ways you couldn't possibly imagine. Things were inserted into the victim's urethra and rectum forcibly. Sometimes, they would insert a glass rod, which Dean and his cohort of abusers would then smash. The pain this would cause is almost too much to comprehend.

At some point during one of their goading sessions, Elmer held a gun to Richard's mouth. This was to terrify the young man, but Elmer pulled the trigger while waving the gun in the victim's face. Richard was shot in the mouth, the bullet shooting straight through and coming out of his neck. This didn't kill him. It just prolonged his agony.

The pair would endure more assaults and torture sessions before being strangled and left beneath the boat shed. In the months that followed, more teen boys would meet the same fate: Willard Branch and Richard Kepner's lives were ended in the most cruel way by Dean, Elmer, and David. In early 1973, Dean moved to another area of Houston, possibly to distance himself from being implicated in the number of boys going missing. He would move several times after this, and there was a lull in his procurement of boys. For four months, the depraved man went without torturing and killing anybody.

It wasn't due to a sudden bout of guilt or remorse. It was down to logistics. Elmer had moved away, telling himself he was done with Dean's revolving door of boys to torture. This meant Dean was a man down.

However, Elmer couldn't stay away for long. Perhaps it was the money that drew him back, or maybe he even missed the thrill of dominance torturing someone. Either way, Elmer helped Dean make up for lost time, and the number of murders was going to escalate rapidly.

By this point, the two accomplices could tell when their leader wanted to pick up a new victim. He'd start pacing around erratically; he'd chain smoke and be visibly on edge. The pair would walk on eggshells around Dean until they brought a new boy in.

William Ray Lawrence, Raymond Blackburn, Homer Garcia, and John Sellars were all abducted, raped, tortured, and killed in quick succession. It seemed the downtime between kills was getting less and less, and Dean's depravity was only on the rise. David Brooks, perhaps looking for a way to step away from Dean slowly, married his girlfriend after finding out she was pregnant.

The summer of 1973 saw Elmer and Dean acting as a duo, adding three more victims to the tally: Michael Baulch, coincidentally the brother of one of their previous victims, Charles Cobble, and Marty Jones.

By that August, David was back on the scene. It seemed like neither boy could stay away for long. Despite the traumas they'd endured, the horrific things they'd seen and done, the lure of Dean, and perhaps his money, called the boys back. These two teens were certainly complicit, and there's no denying their guilt and heavy involvement in the crimes, but to me, they were trauma-bonded to the older man. Neither teen knew how to sever the ties they had to Dean, and no matter how much they tried to cut the cord, they couldn't do it.

On August 3, David acquired his last ever victim for Dean, 13-year-old James Dreymala. The young boy was riding his bike on a sunny afternoon when David bought him a pizza and chatted with him for about an hour. David was grooming the child - much like Dean had done to him - and readying him to be taken to the house of horrors.

Once lured back to the property, the little blond boy endured the same as all the other boys before him. It's such a heartbreaking thought that prior to that afternoon, the worst pain this child had felt was from falling off his bike. The things he was forced to endure before his death are a testament to just how sick Dean Corll was. Once the evil man was done with the boy, he wrapped a cord around his neck while he was still strapped to the plywood torture board and strangled him to death. James would end up beneath the boat house.

A few days later, Elmer invited a friend to Dean's house to drink, which Timothy Kerley gladly accepted. It would seem as though Elmer was eying his friend up to be another victim, although at 20 years old, he may have been too old for Dean's liking. Still, the three of them sat and enjoyed drinks on the night of August 7, which rolled into the early hours of August 8. The trio began sniffing paint before Elmer and Tim decided to take a drive out. "We'll be back soon," Elmer promised Dean, who would be left alone for a few hours.

The young men headed to Houston Heights, where Elmer was living, but as they pulled up, they heard awful screaming coming from the house across the street. It was a girl's cry for help, after which they saw their friend, Rhonda Williams, hobble from her family home in tears. Her father had beaten her after getting drunk, not an unheard occurrence for the 15-year-old. "Hey, get in," Elmer shouted to the teen, rescuing her from the wrath of her father - but in doing so, introducing her to the evil of Dean Corll.

The three headed back to Corll's residence, by which point it was 3:00 a.m.

As soon as Dean saw the young girl in tow, he flew off in a rage, screaming at Elmer, spitting at him that he'd ruined everything. Elmer tried his best to explain the girl was getting beat on by her father and had nowhere else to go. Plus, she was his friend and wasn't safe. An incensed Dean took some time to cool down, which he eventually did. His mood lifted. He offered his guests a toke and some beers, which they all accepted. Elmer and Tim also began inhaling paint fumes, and before long, the three of them were passed out. The only person who was wide awake was Dean.

The sun was coming up, and light was making its way through the window slats. Dean hadn't slept. He was sitting looking at the trio of youths sprawled in his home. While they were asleep, he'd tied them all up. Rope bound their hands and feet while tape covered their mouths. Dean had removed all of Tim's clothes prior to securing his limbs with rope.

The three lay next to one another, slowly awakening from their slumbers. Elmer woke first, and Dean walked over and ripped the tape from his mouth; again, he began yelling at the teenager for bringing back a girl. There was nothing Elmer could say to pacify the man, who admitted all three of them were going to die. After, of course, he'd abused them. "I'm gonna have my fun," Dean spat as he waved a pistol around.

He awoke Rhonda by kicking her multiple times before pulling Elmer to his feet. "I'll help you kill them," Elmer reasoned, begging Dean to set him free. If he did, he'd do as Dean asked: torture and kill the others. Eventually, the pair came to an agreement, and Elmer was set free. They then carried the victims to the bedroom, where they were both bound to the torture board. Tim was tied down face first, while Rhonda was facing upwards, able to see what her attackers were planning.

Dean tossed his protégé a knife. "Cut off her clothes," he demanded. Elmer agreed and began slicing the teen's garments from her. Dean ordered the teen to rape the girl while he abused Tim. Elmer agreed, and Dean began violently beating Tim, who was now wide awake. He was still gagged, but Elmer had removed Rhonda's tape, and she pulled him close, asking him if this was really happening. "Yes," he said.

The defiant girl told him to do something about it. This sprung Elmer into action for whatever reason, and he turned and took hold of Dean's pistol. "You've gone far enough," he warned as Dean abused his victim. Elmer raised his voice, desperate for Dean to listen to him. "Kill me!" Dean goaded the teen as he held the pistol in front of him. Dean didn't take Elmer's threat seriously and began making his way toward him to swipe the pistol from him, screaming all the while.

Elmer shot at Dean, and the bullet hit him in the head. It wasn't enough to stop him from walking toward Elmer, though, just like a horror movie villain who'd been shot fatally but still managed to continue attacking their victim. Elmer fired another shot, then another, one of which penetrated Dean's shoulder. Realizing the teen was serious, the wounded man retreated and tried to run away, but Elmer shot him three more times. Dean slumped next to his hallway wall and slid down it, unable to walk any further. Blood smeared the wall as he slipped, and his back was seeping with blood from the bullets that had just pierced him.

Stark naked, lying in his own blood, Dean Corll died almost immediately.

Elmer was in shock. He'd just killed the person he looked up to. The man who'd been a big brother to him, who'd made sure he was never short of money, who gave him the time of day. A thought popped up for the teen: Dean would have been so proud of how I managed this situation. Even after his death, Elmer was still seeking Dean's approval.

Rhonda and Tim were untied, and the trio had an emotional encounter, with Tim thanking his friend for saving his life. They talked about what they should do. Elmer wanted to leave and forget it ever happened, but the other two disagreed. They wanted to call the police. Just before 8:30 that morning, Elmer called 911, and he confessed to killing Dean Corll.

The three then sat outside on Dean's porch, watching the day break as they waited for the police to arrive. As they did, Elmer said something peculiar to Tim. "If you weren't my friend," he sighed, "I could have got $200 for you."

All teens were taken into custody, and their stories all tied in with one another. It was a clear case of self-defense, police thought, and it seemed like an open-and-shut case. Until Elmer began confessing.

He told investigators that he and an accomplice, David Brooks, had been acquiring young boys for Dean for the past few years. The reason for this was for Dean to torture, rape, and kill them. He offered the whereabouts of the victims, most of whom were underneath the boat shed.

The police thought it was drug-induced rambling. They thought the boy was still high and didn't read too much into his outlandish claims. Until he mentioned the names of some of the victims. These boys had been reported missing, presumed runaways, but if what Elmer was telling them was true, they were victims of one of the worst serial killers to exist.

A more thorough look at Dean Corll's property showed the boy might be telling the truth. They found the torture board. The floor had a sheet of clear plastic covering it. Dean also owned a lot of dubious items: handcuffs, sex toys, various lengths of rope, and hunting knives. Separately, these items aren't anything to think twice about. Bundle them together, and you have to consider how the owner of these items is using them.

Elmer eventually took the police to the boat shed. He was telling the truth. Among the bodies were bags of clothing that had belonged to the boys. The faces of the victims were haunting. One boy's mouth was wide open, so much so you could see his top and bottom teeth. It was clear he'd died while screaming at the top of his lungs.

Elmer had implicated David Brooks, who willingly spoke with police. He denied everything Elmer had said but did admit he knew Dean had raped and killed two boys years earlier. This contradicted everything Elmer had admitted so far, and as far as police could tell, the boy had been truthful. He'd guided them to where the bodies were; the method of murder was always right, and the utilization of torture was always accurate, too. Elmer admitted to being involved in nine murders and insisted David Brooks was involved in most of these, too.

After hours of interrogation, David cracked. He does not give the full truth but begins admitting to helping Dean and Elmer bury the bodies, but denies actively torturing or killing anyone. *Didn't seeing those dead boys bother him*, the police asked. No, David admitted. Eventually, the police managed to get the teen to take them to the grave sites of some of the victims who'd been buried at High Island Beach.

A total of 28 bodies had been recovered. The boys were remanded, and their bond was set at $100,000. It was agreed that Elmer wouldn't face a murder charge for the murder of Dean Corll as it was deemed self-defense. He was brought to trial in the summer of 1974, and he was found guilty of six murders. Elmer got 99 years in jail. David was only found guilty of one murder, but that was enough to put him behind bars for life.

Elmer is eligible for parole in late 2025. David died, aged 65, in 2020.

This case is as intriguing as it is sickening. The fact that Corll managed to convince not just one but two young boys to carry out torture killings with him is darkly fascinating. The fact he got away with his crimes for so long, and no doubt would have if he weren't murdered, is terrifying.

This story begins with two vulnerable teenage boys seeking a father figure or older brother-type friend to help guide their way. Elmer was bullied by his father and David was bullied by just about everyone. Dean noticed the boys' vulnerabilities and used them to his own sick advantage, turning them both into monsters, just like he was.